A JOURNEY TO OHIO IN 1810

A JOURNEY TO OHIO
IN 1810

As Recorded in the Journal of
Margaret Van Horn Dwight

Edited with an Introduction by Max Farrand

Introduction to the Bison Book Edition by Jay Gitlin

University of Nebraska Press
Lincoln and London

First Bison Book printing: 1991
Most recent printing indicated by the first digit below:
10   9   8   7   6   5   4   3   2   1

Library of Congress Cataloging-in-Publication Data
Dwight, Margaret Van Horn, 1790–1834.
A journey to Ohio in 1810: as recorded in the journal of Margaret Van Horn Dwight / edited with an introduction by Max Farrand; introduction to the Bison Book edition by Jay Gitlin.
p. cm.
Reprint. Originally published: New Haven: Yale University Press, 1913.
ISBN 0-8032-6589-1
1. United States—Description and travel—1783–1848.
2. Atlantic States—Description and travel.   3. Pennsylvania—Description and travel.   4. Ohio—Description and travel.   5. Dwight, Margaret Van Horn, 1790–1834—Diaries.   I. Farrand, Max, 1860–1945.
II. Title.
E164.D96   1991
917.3—dc20
91-14171   CIP

Reprinted from the 1912 edition published by Yale University Press

We Americans like to think of ourselves as a restless
people, a nation of hardy souls who have relished a good
adventure from the days of covered wagons to the voy-
ages of the Starship Enterprise. Then there are those like
my mother who, while watching the first manned space
flight, turned to her family and asked, "How do they go to
the bathroom?" Reading Margaret Van Horn Dwight's
journal reminded me of my mother's comment.
Throughout her journey to Ohio, Dwight expressed her
displeasure over the lack of amenities on the trail. Here
we have one pioneer not about to accept discomfort without a struggle or, at least, a cutting remark. Describing
her lodgings for one night in Pennsylvania, Dwight noted
that the place had "a floor containing dirt enough to plant
potatoes."

Margaret Dwight's journal of her trip from Milford,
Connecticut, to Warren, Ohio, in 1810 is the kind of document that historians ransack musty archives hoping to
find, usually without success. Dwight's journal gives us a
first-hand account that goes way beyond the usual reckoning of miles traveled and notes on the weather. Dwight
provides an intimate view of the people she met along the
way. From her observations we get a sense of the backcountry settlements of Pennsylvania and Ohio in this period, the language, the sounds, and even the smells of this
early American frontier. This would be a valuable and
rare document if only because it furnishes a woman's perspective on a western passage that has received little attention from historians. As an added bonus, it is a journal

full of witty—Margaret might have described herself as a "clever girl"—and occasionally sarcastic remarks.

Margaret Dwight was indeed no simple young woman. She was born on December 29, 1790, into one of the most prominent families in New England. Her grandfather, Major Timothy Dwight of Northampton, Massachusetts, was a successful merchant and judge. A giant of a man for the times, his 6′4″ stature matched his standing in the community. He married Mary Edwards, the daughter of Jonathan Edwards, Anglo-America's first great religious philosopher. Margaret's father, Doctor Maurice William Dwight, died at age thirty in 1796 during a yellow fever epidemic. It was a tragic year for the family as two of Margaret's younger siblings also died, leaving only Margaret, the eldest child; Maurice, Jr. the youngest; and their mother, Margaret Dewitt Dwight of Milford, Connecticut. When their mother subsequently remarried, Margaret was sent to Northampton to be raised by her grandmother.

A relative described Margaret's grandmother, Mary Edwards Dwight, as a "very strong-minded woman [with] quite superior instincts and habits of analytic thought. Her most striking mental traits were her quick habits of observation, and her thorough and keen analysis of men and things. She had strong prepossessions and prejudices." Though we have no such descriptions of Margaret Dwight herself, it seems clear from a reading of her journal that she was heavily influenced by her grandmother. When her grandmother died in 1807, Margaret went to New Haven to live with the family of her father's younger sister, Elizabeth Dwight, who had married William Walton Woolsey. Aunt Elizabeth was described as intelligent, thoughtful, and fond of poetry. Margaret Dwight was trained by educated women, women who may well have considered themselves the intellectual equals of the most educated men of the time. This was, of course, a family with unusually high standards. Margaret's uncle, Timothy Dwight, was the president of Yale from 1795 to 1817. Her cousin, Theodore Dwight Woolsey, was the president of Yale from 1846 to 1871. Her own brother, Maurice, became the Reverend Doctor of the First Reformed Dutch Church of Brooklyn, New York, and was known as a good preacher, a tall, genial, and liberal-minded man.[1]

It was naturally with great reluctance that Margaret took leave of such accomplished and loving relations. So she tells us in the first page of her journal, written for her cousin and friend, Elizabeth Woolsey. Exactly why Margaret decided to travel to Ohio in 1810 we do not know. We do know, however, that Ohio was considered a land of opportunity not only by farmers looking to exchange the rocky soil of New England for cheaper, more fertile land in the West, but also by the sons and daughters of prominent New England families, hoping to secure positions of political and social authority in developing communities. Margaret was, in fact, going to live with the family of her cousin, Joseph Woodbridge, who had settled in Warren, Ohio, in the Western Reserve.

A number of young Connecticut gentlemen had relocated to Ohio to serve as agents and promoters for the various investors in the lands of the Western or Connecticut Reserve. When the state of Connecticut ceded its claim to western lands to the United States in 1786, it reserved a tract containing some 3.5 million acres. This tract, the Western Reserve, was bounded in the North by the international line between Canada and the United States; in the South, by the 41st parallel of north latitude; in the East, by the western boundary of Pennsylvania; in the West, by a line parallel to and 120 miles west of that

Pennsylvania border. In 1792 the Connecticut General Assembly set aside a tract of 500,000 acres at the western end of the Reserve to compensate citizens of towns like Danbury, New Haven, and New London that had suffered from British depredations during the War for Independence. This tract became known as "The Sufferers' Lands," or the "Firelands." In 1795 Connecticut authorized the sale of the rest of the Reserve for not less than a million dollars, the proceeds to benefit the Connecticut School Fund. Later that year, the entire parcel of some three million acres was sold for 1.2 million dollars to an association of fifty-eight investors operating as the Connecticut Land Company.

Speculation in western lands had long been a preoccupation of men with capital and connections. Margaret Dwight's grandfather, Major Timothy Dwight, had died in Mississippi in 1777 while pursuing his investment and that of his widowed sister, Eleanor Lyman, in a huge land grant and proposed colony near Natchez. When the Revolutionary War came to a close, interest in western lands reached new heights. Both state and national governments sought to finance their debts and pay war veterans through the sale or exchange of the governments' principal asset, backcountry acres. Speculative fever reached a climax in the period from 1786 to 1796. The Ohio Company purchased land in southeastern Ohio in 1787. The associates of the Connecticut Land Company began to sell off the Western Reserve after surveys were completed in 1796 and 1797. A group of Dutch bankers formed the Holland Land Company and purchased over three million acres of land in western New York State in 1792 and began sales in 1800. The United States Government became a serious competitor in the retail sale of western lands after the passage of the Land Law of 1800, which established more convenient district land offices in the West, extended credit to purchasers, and reduced the minimum tract purchasable to 320 acres.

With so much land on the market, the competition among the sellers was rather fierce. Although most travelers, including Margaret Dwight, reported heavy traffic on the roads leading to Ohio, the demand could not keep up with the supply, and the land market, especially in areas away from the major river arteries, was sluggish until after the War of 1812. Speculators who wished to turn a profit learned quickly that they must become developers. To facilitate the sale of land and attract settlers, developers paid for surveys and took out advertisements to promote the virtues of their real estate. They built roads and encouraged through incentives the establishment of taverns, sawmills, and gristmills on their tracts. Eastern investment and western development were intimately connected. The notion that the frontier somehow developed in isolation would have seemed a bitter joke to many Connecticut investors.

The experience of the Connecticut Land Company is instructive. First, the associates paid for a survey that imposed an abstract grid on the land. An orderly system of townships five miles square, grouped and numbered from east to west in ranges, eased the transfer and location of property and minimized confusion and litigation over claims. In 1797 and 1798 the associates spent over $4,000 for roads. By 1800 the Connecticut Land Company had laid out $100,000 in interest payments and $80,000 for improvements. Yet there were only some one thousand inhabitants in the Reserve spread out over thirty-five settlements, and few, if any, investors had seen any profit from their lands.

The misfortunes of the Connecticut Land Company

flowed from two main problems. First, the company suffered from bad management and a fatal flaw in its opera-
tions. From the time of its first division of lands in 1798,
the company in reality became nothing more than a collection of private investors. The associates competed with
each other for sales. Although some pooled their re-
sources and shared expenses, the lack of a unified vision
and plan for the Reserve undoubtedly contributed to the
company's demise. Pricing policies varied from one
township to the next. Moreover, many investors re-
mained in Connecticut and never appreciated conditions
in Ohio. One large investor, Margaret Dwight's great-un-
cle, Pierpont Edwards, sent his son, John S. Edwards, to
Ohio to act as his agent. John S. Edwards, who greeted
Margaret upon her arrival in Ohio, achieved some success as a local political leader. He was elected to Congress
in 1812; however, he was never able to interest many settlers in Mesopotamia, Ohio, the center of his father's
holdings. When his son died in 1813, Pierpont Edwards
turned to a succession of agents, none of whom he ever
trusted. They, in turn, complained to him that his land
was priced above the surrounding lands belonging to his
competitors.

Sellers were forced to offer lower prices and more lib-
eral credit terms throughout the first decade of the nine-
teenth century. Demand for land in the Reserve increased after 1815, due in part to depressed economic
conditions in New England and the summer frosts in that
region in 1816. But expansion in the West was short-
lived. The Bank of the United States reversed its infla-
tionary policies in the summer of 1818, and a financial
crisis, the Panic of 1819, ensued. Cash, always scarce on
the frontier, all but disappeared. The prices of agri-
cultural products fell dramatically, barely covering the

costs of transportation for western producers. Here was the source of the Connecticut Land Company's other main problem. Until the completion of the Erie Canal in 1825 and the subsequent construction of the Ohio Canal linking the Ohio River with Lake Erie, the Western Reserve would remain an economic backwater. Its farmers had no cost-efficient way of getting their products to market and, therefore, had little cash to pay off their mortgages.[2]

The importance of linkages throughout the history of American expansion from Ohio to Alaska can hardly be overemphasized. For six weeks, Margaret Dwight was surrounded by travelers, teamsters, and innkeepers. This was not a passage through the wilderness. It was simply a bumpy ride over rough roads. Through Dwight's descriptions, we observe the transition from frontier to region, we see the process of forming and maintaining connections in a newly-settled area. There were the personal connections. As Margaret notes after her arrival in Warren, "A cousin in this country, is not to be slighted I assure you—I would give more for one in this country, than for 20 in old Connecticut." As in Margaret's case, destinations were often predetermined by the prior settlement of relatives. Families and groups of neighbors traveled west. Sons were sent by fathers to look after their investments. It is a cliché to point out the influence of New England and especially Connecticut on the culture of the Western Reserve. Perhaps it is only a more obvious example of a phenomenon we have underemphasized when writing the histories of other frontier areas. Preexisting relationships did indeed influence the formation of frontier societies.

The other connections that influenced the shape of development were geographical: the transportation net-

works that carried people, produce, and merchandise between frontier settlements and the markets and
population centers of the East Coast. Before the opening
of the Erie Canal, the most important network in the Old
Northwest was the Ohio and Mississippi river system,
which flowed to the west and the south. Travelers from
the east heading for Ohio in 1810 relied on two land
routes, the northern Genesee Road through New York
and the southern Forbes' Road through Pennsylvania.
Yankee emigrants using the northern route might cross
the Hudson River at Newburgh, New York, travel
through Binghamton and Ithaca, and pick up the main
road around Geneva. Most followed the Mohawk Valley
past Albany and headed west for Utica, where they
picked up the Genesee Road. The Genesee route was rel-
atively flat and emigrants could travel as many as thirty
miles a day. By the 1840s one could take the railroad from
Boston to Albany, follow the Erie canal to Buffalo, and
take a steamboat on Lake Erie to Ohio. A trip requiring
four to six weeks had been reduced to one of several days'
duration.

Margaret Dwight's party took the southern route.
They followed the Connecticut coastline through Milford and Fairfield, ferried across the Hudson, and traveled through Morristown and Chester in central New Jersey. Crossing a covered bridge over the Delaware around
Easton, the party then made its way through the Pennsylvania Dutch towns of Bethlehem, Kutztown, and
Lebanon, reaching Harrisburg two weeks after leaving
Connecticut. From Carlisle to Pittsburgh, some two hundred miles, Dwight's group followed the Pennsylvania
State Road, an upgrade of the old Forbes' Road. Travelers heading for Marietta in southeastern Ohio might
have taken the left fork four miles beyond Bedford,

Pennsylvania. This road, the old Glade Road, was reported by Dwight to be ten times worse than the right fork her party had taken, something Dwight thought impossible to imagine. The right fork crossed the Allegheny Mountains to Greensburg and Pittsburgh. From there, the road followed the Ohio, Beaver, and Mahoning rivers into Ohio. The entire trip took Dwight's party six weeks. Margaret walked much of the way over the mountains, and the party averaged little more than ten miles a day. Again, these conditions did not last very long. By 1834 travelers were able to traverse Pennsylvania using a combination of railroads, canals, and stagecoach lines.[3]

Crude conditions notwithstanding, the roads linking Ohio to the East were dotted with taverns or inns. A friend of Margaret Dwight, Henry Ellsworth, traveled much the same route in 1811 and reported that

In every town a stranger is astonished to find so many taverns. You never need inquire *where* there is a tavern, for you may at a great distance see the large signs projected out into the highway apparently half across it.[4]

Another traveler reported that Pittsburgh contained twenty-four taverns in 1807, five of them excellent. Margaret Dwight undoubtedly missed the better inns, for the family she was traveling with, Deacon Wolcott, his wife, their daughter Susan and son Erastus, stayed in the more inexpensive, "country" taverns. As Margaret confides in her journal, "If I am caught with a Deacon of any name, again, I shall deserve to suffer." Henry Ellsworth also noted the presence of beer shops along the route, claiming to find "these drachm [dram] shops every mile or two to Pittsburgh" after crossing the Connecticut border. The beer shops were apparently not patronized by Dwight's party.

The beer shops were frequented, however, by wagoners or teamsters hauling goods back and forth over these hard roads. With their Conestoga wagons and Conestoga cigars or stogies, the ubiquitous wagoners were in the business of linking East and West and were a constant reminder of the importance of commerce. The wagoners certainly made an unfavorable impression on Margaret Dwight, who mentions them on many pages of her journal. After several annoying incidents, she finally records coming upon an "Irish waggoner" who seems to be a "well inform'd man—& what is more, has read his bible . . . I think I will never condemn a whole race again—I can now, even believe it possible to find a clever Dutchman in Pennsylvania."[5]

Readers will note that Dwight obviously had her prejudices. Her descriptions of the Pennsylvania Dutch—Germans, not Hollanders—underscore the profoundly ethnic character of many backcountry settlements. Like many Yankees, Dwight admired German barns, but was quite unimpressed by German houses, the dress of German women, and the general frivolity on the Sabbath in German settlements. Above all, Dwight was simply uncomfortable around people so different from herself. Upon reaching Harrisburg, she wrote with a distinct sense of relief, "We have once more got among people of our own nation & language."

Readers should also be aware that Dwight's journal provides only a partial picture of the activities on this frontier. Her party spent little time in the larger towns along the route, and Margaret herself seems to have had little interest in mercantile matters. Her friend Henry Ellsworth, on the other hand, noted prices and commercial prospects throughout his journal. He spent four days in Pittsburgh visiting banks, foundries, and mills.

Margaret's journal does, however, provide us with valuable and refreshing observations on women. Women of all types appear on these pages, from the "2 young women, whom I thought *amazoons*" that kept a tavern in New Jersey to a "poor black girl" mistreated by a landlord's pretentious sister. Dwight not only observes other women, she supplies a woman's perspective and has experiences on the trip that only a woman could have. She felt threatened on several occasions and suffered a rather serious assault on her privacy in bed one night by a drunken wagoner. On a more humorous note, she observed one man traveling west who was full of "pompous speeches." With sarcasm befitting a young woman who was the intellectual superior of many men who presumed the opposite, Margaret noted that this man's "language is very ungrammatical—but the Jacksons [some traveling companions] are all in raptures with him . . . I could make them believe . . . that I was a girl of great larnin—if I were to say over Kermogenious—Heterogenious & a few such words without any connection—no matter if I do but bring them in some how."

One persistent subject throughout the journal is marriage and husbands. It is a subject often brought up by others. In New York, Margaret notes: "She said I should never come back alone, that I would certainly be married in a little while." In New Jersey: "There was a man to day . . . who enquired, or rather *expected* we were going to the Hio—we told him yes & he at once concluded it was to get husbands." The subject, of course, was on the mind of twenty-year-old Margaret Dwight. Several times in the journal, she mentions two judges, Dobson and Stephenson, apparently young Connecticut men in Ohio, as potential mates. At one point she confesses that she "may be willing to descend from a judge to a blacksmith" but is determined to wait until she arrives in Warren: "It is clever to have two or three strings to ones bow." While her expectations generally seem to be a source of some gaiety, there is also more than a hint of anxiety in the mix. After meeting a young lady returning from a year spent in Warren, Ohio *unmarried* [her emphasis], Margaret says, "I feel quite encouraged by it & do not believe the place as dangerous as is generally reported."

In fact, Margaret Dwight did marry William Bell, a dry-goods merchant born in Ireland, a little over a year after her arrival in Ohio. Earlier that year, her Connecticut friend Ellsworth spent several hours chatting with her in Warren and reported her as being in good health and "pleased with her new situation." Margaret left Ohio and moved with her husband and several young children to Pittsburgh around 1815. (Margaret's mother also came to Pittsburgh to live.) The couple had thirteen children, ten of whom lived to adulthood. The two oldest sons became manufacturers. Three daughters married men of substantial means in St. Louis. Two other sons became partners in a Pittsburgh law practice; another became a doctor. The two youngest daughters married ministers. A grandson, Maurice Dwight Collier, returned to Connecticut and graduated from Yale in 1866. And so the circle was completed. Margaret Dwight died a month after the birth of her thirteenth child in 1834 at the age of 45.

Throughout her journey, Margaret Dwight maintained a rather disdainful view of western customs, morals, speech, and accommodations. In a classic statement that provides some comic relief to our traditional belief in the pioneer spirit, Margaret wrote, "We have concluded the reason so few are willing to return from the Western country, is not that the country is so good, but because the journey is so bad." Yet, even Margaret

Dwight, like many other Americans before and after her, began to derive some satisfaction from her westering experience. The same day she penned the lines quoted above, she wrote: "I have learn'd Elizabeth, to eat raw *pork* & drink whisky—dont you think I shall do for a new country?"

Note on the text: Margaret Dwight sent her journal to her cousin, Elizabeth Woolsey, as soon as she reached Ohio. Many years later the journal was given to a son of the author and subsequently was in the possession of a granddaughter, Katharine Reynolds Wishart of Waterford, Pennsylvania. Historian Max Farrand consulted the original at that point and prepared the text for publication. It was first published by the Yale University Press in 1912. Two independent handwritten copies of the journal were made, possibly by a member of the Woolsey family. One resides at the Manuscripts and Archives division of the Yale University Library. The original journal is now held by the Western Reserve Historical Society. Farrand provided no footnotes in the original edition; however, few words or references require explanation. There are several archaic usages: "baiting" the horses meant feeding them during the trip; "stoning" the raisins meant removing the pits. Cherry bounce was a drink made from cherries, sugar, and whiskey. Brandy sling was simply sweetened brandy, often lemon-flavored.

NOTES

1. Information about Margaret Dwight and the Dwight family comes from an annotated copy of Benjamin W. Dwight, *The History of the Descendants of John Dwight of Dedham, Massachusetts,* 2 vols. (New York: John F. Trow and Son, 1874), located in Manuscripts and Archives, Yale University Library. My thanks to Judith Schiff, Chief Research Archivist, for bringing this volume to my attention. Brooks M. Kelley, *Yale: A History* (New Haven: Yale University Press, 1974) is the standard one-volume history

of this institution. A recent discussion of women's literacy in New England—Joel Perlmann and Dennis Shirley, "When Did New England Women Acquire Literacy?" *William and Mary Quarterly,* 3d Ser. (January 1991): 48:1—suggests that we have underestimated the extent of such literacy in the late colonial period and that the proportion of younger New England women with some education increased substantially as early as 1780.

2. This brief historical sketch of the Western Reserve and the Ohio frontier has been drawn from the following works: Claude L. Shepard, *The Connecticut Land Company: A Study in the Beginnings of Colonization of the Western Reserve,* The Western Reserve Historical Society, Annual Report for 1915–1916, Tract No. 96, Part II (Cleveland: WRHS, 1916); Harlan Hatcher, *The Western Reserve* (Indianapolis: Bobbs-Merrill, 1949); William T. Utter, *The Frontier State, 1803–1825,* Volume 2 of The History of the State of Ohio, ed. Carl Wittke (Columbus: Ohio State Archaeological and Historical Society, 1942); Pierpont Edwards Papers, Manuscripts and Archives, Yale University Library. (Brian Harte has kindly shared his knowledge of this collection.) Harry F. Lupold and Gladys Haddad, eds., *Ohio's Western Reserve* (Kent, Ohio: Kent State University Press, 1988) is a convenient and excellent collection of recent scholarly articles. Andrew R. L. Cayton, *The Frontier Republic* (Kent, Ohio: Kent State University Press, 1986) provides a subtle and informative rethinking of the political history of Ohio in its formative period. See William Wyckoff, *The Developer's Frontier: The Making of the Western New York Landscape* (New Haven: Yale University Press, 1988) contains an excellent discussion of the role of land developers in the process of frontier settlement.

3. Archer B. Hulbert, *The Old Glade (Forbes) Road (Pennsylvania State Road),* Historic Highways of America, vol. 5 (Cleveland: Arthur H. Clark, 1903); John W. Harpster, ed., *Crossroads: Descriptions of Western Pennsylvania, 1720–1829* (Pittsburgh: University of Pittsburgh Press, 1938; reprint edition, 1986). John J. Horton, *The Jonathan Hale Farm* (Cleveland: The Western Reserve Historical Society, 1961) has a nice description of one pioneer's travels on the northern route to Ohio.

4. This quote and two that follow are taken from Phillip R. Shriver, *A Tour to New Connecticut in 1811: The Narrative of Henry*

Leavitt Ellsworth (Cleveland: Western Reserve Historical Society, 1985). Shriver supplies a fine introduction and very useful endnotes.

5. James M. Miller, *The Genesis of Western Culture: The Upper Ohio Valley, 1800–1825* (New York: Da Capo Press, 1969, originally published in 1938) supplies information on taverns and teamsters in this period. John D. Unruh, Jr., *The Plains Across* (Urbana: University of Illinois Press, 1979) shows the importance of supply services provided by private entrepreneurs at their trading posts along the routes to California and Oregon in a later period.

INTRODUCTION

"If it be true that good wine needs no bush, 'tis true that a good play needs no epilogue;" and Rosalind might well have added that a good story needs no prologue. The present journal is complete in itself, and it is such a perfect gem, that it seems a pity to mar its beauty by giving it any but the simplest setting. There are many readers, however, with enough human interest to wish to know who Rosalind really was, and to be assured that she "married and lived happily ever after." That is the reason for this introduction.

Margaret Van Horn Dwight was born on December 29, 1790. She was the daughter of Doctor Maurice William Dwight, a brother of President Timothy Dwight of Yale, and Margaret (DeWitt) Dwight. The death of her father in 1796, and the subsequent marriage of her mother, was probably the reason for Margaret Dwight being taken by her grandmother, Mary Edwards Dwight, a daughter of Jonathan Edwards, who trained her as her own child in her family in Northampton. The death of her grandmother, February 7, 1807, was the occasion of her going to live in New Haven in the family of her aunt, Elizabeth Dwight, who had married William Walton Woolsey, and whose son was President Theodore Woolsey.

Three years later, in 1810, Margaret Dwight left New Haven to go to her cousins in Warren, Ohio.

INTRODUCTION

It was doubtless there that she met Mr. Bell, whom she married, December 17, 1811, a year after her arrival. William Bell, Jr., was born in Ireland, February 11, 1781, and after 1815 he was a wholesale merchant in Pittsburgh.

The family genealogy formally records that Margaret Dwight Bell became the mother of thirteen children, that she died on October 9, 1834, and that she was "a lady of remarkable sweetness and excellence, and devotedly religious." Family tradition adds a personal touch in relating that her home was a center of hospitality and that she herself was active and very vivacious.

The journal of the rough wagon trip to Ohio in 1810 was evidently kept by Margaret Dwight in fulfilment of a promise to her cousin, Elizabeth Woolsey, to whom it was sent as soon as the journey was over. A good many years later the journal was given to a son of the author, and the original is now in the possession of a granddaughter, Miss Katharine Reynolds Wishart of Waterford, Pennsylvania. It has been well cared for and is in excellent condition, except that the first two pages are missing. This is of less importance from the fact that two independent copies had been made. The text of the journal here printed is taken from the original manuscript, and is reproduced as accurately as typographical devices permit.

MAX FARRAND.

A JOURNEY TO OHIO

Margaret Dwight traveled this route in 1810.

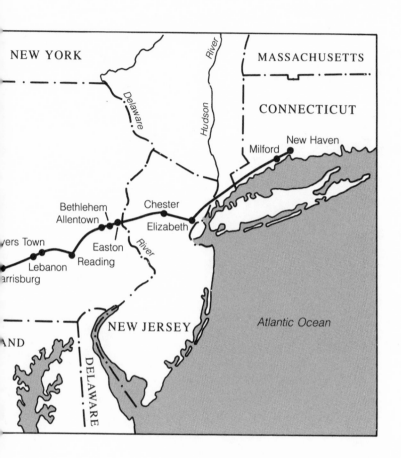

A JOURNEY TO OHIO

Milford Friday Eve. at Capt Pond's.

Shall I commence my journal, my dear Elizabeth, with a description of the pain I felt at taking leave of all my friends, or shall I leave you to imagine?— The afternoon has been spent by me in the most painful reflections & in almost total silence by my companions— I have thought of a thousand things unsaid, a thousand kindnesses unpaid with thanks that I ought to have remembered more seasonably; and the neglect of which causes me many uneasy feelings— my neglecting to take leave of Sally, has had the same effect— I hope she did not feel hurt by it, for it proceeded from no want of gratitude for her kindness to me. I did not imagine parting with any friend could be so distressing as I found leaving your Mama. I did not know till then, how much I loved her & could I at that moment have retraced my steps! but it was too late to repent— Deacon Wolcott & his wife are very kind, obliging, people, & Miss Wolcott is a very pleasant companion, I do not know what I should do without her. We came on to Butler's this afternoon & I came immediately down to Uncle Pond's & drank tea. Miss W. came with me & both Uncle & Aunt invited her to stay and sleep with me, which she accordingly did. Cousin Patty has been with me, to say good bye, to all my friends, & to-morrow we proceed to Stamford.

Sat. night, D. Nash's Inn. Middlesex–

We had a cold, unsociable ride today, each one of us being occupied in thinking of the friends we had left behind & of the distance, which was every moment increasing, between them & us. Mrs W has left an aged father in the last stages of consumption, that was a sufficient excuse for silence on her part. Mr W. made several attempts to dispel & by kind words & *phebeish** looks but without success; he appears to be a very fond husband. We stopt to *eat oats* at a Tavern in Fairfield, West Farms, an old Lady came into the room where Miss W. (whose name, by the way, is Susan, not Hannah, Sally, or Abby) & we were sitting. "Well! Gals where are you going?" "To New Connecticut" "You bant tho– To New Connecticut? Why what a long journey! do you ever expect to get there? How far is it?" "Near 600 miles" "Well Gals, you Gals & your husbands with you?" "No Ma'am"– "Not got your husbands! Well I don't know– they say there's wild Indians there!" The poor woman was then call'd out to her daughter (the mistress of the house) who she told us has been ill five months with a swelling & she had come that afternoon to see it

---

*For the description of the word *Phebeish*, the reader is referred to Miss Julia.

launch'd by the Physicians who were then in the house— She went out but soon return'd & told us they were "cutting her poor child all to pieces"- She did not know but she should as lieve see a wild Indian as to see that scene over again— I felt very sorry for the poor old Lady- I could not help smiling at the comparison. The country we pass thro' till we are beyond N. York, I need not describe to you, nor indeed could I; for I am attended by a very unpleasant tho' not uncommon, companion- one to whom I have bow'd in subjection ever since I left you–Pride— It has entirely prevented my seeing the country lest I should be known— You will cry "for shame" & so did I but it did no good- I could neither shame nor reason it away, & so I suppose it will attend me to the mountains, then I am sure it will bid me adieu- "for you know the proverb" 'pride dwelleth not among the mountains'- I don't certainly know where this proverb is to be found, but Julia can tell you- for if I mistake not it is on the next page to "There is nothing sweet" &c- I do not find it so unpleasant riding in a waggon as I expected- nor am I very much fatigued with it- but four weeks to ride all the time, is fatigueing to think of- We came on to Nash's tavern where we found no company excepting one gentleman who looks like a Dr Susannah (Mr Nash's granddaughter) says he is a "particular bit" one who likes good eating & a great deal of waiting upon, better than he likes to pay for it- Here we stay over the Sabbath.

A JOURNEY TO OHIO

Sunday eve—

This morning Susannah came & invited us to attend meeting– we at first refused but I afterwards chang'd my mind, & "took a notion" (as Susannah told her friends to whom she did me the honour to introduce me) to go– so taking an apple to eat on the road we set out for the church– It was "situated on an eminence" but was a small old wooden building– The minister; who I found was brother to Mr Fisher, Susannah told me was not very well liked by some "he hadn't so good a gait to deliver his sermons as some," but she believ'd he was a very serious good man– She then gave me his history but I cannot spend time to give it to you– – The sermon had nothing very striking in it but if I had time I would write you the text heads &c just to let you see I remember it, though I fear it has done me no good for I heard it like a stranger and did not realize that I was interested in it *at* all– I was entirely of Susannah's opinion respecting the preacher, for I thought his "gait to deliver" was better than his voice, for he has a most terrible *nasal twang*— Before we got home at noon, I had found out the squire & half the parish, Susannah's history & many other *interesting* things which I have almost forgotten— I saw 4 or 5 well dress'd good looking girls, & as many young men answering the first part of the description, one of whom was chorister– & another, from the resemblance he bears them, I imagine must be brother to Miss Haines or the N York

Sexton— I went all day to meeting & am now very tir'd, for our walk was a very long one, I should think almost 2 miles each way which would make almost 4 miles for one poor sermon——

October 22– Monday– Cook's inn—

County West Chester–

I never will go to New Connecticut with a *Deacon* again, for we put up at every byeplace in the country to *save expence*– It is very grating to my pride to go into a tavern & furnish & cook my own provision– to ride in a wagon &c &c– but that I can possibly get along with– but to be oblig'd to pass the night in such a place as we are now in, just because it is a little cheaper, is more than I am willing to do– I should even rather drink clear rum out of the wooden bottle after the deacon has drank & wip'd it over with his hand, than to stay here another night—— The house is very small & very dirty– it serves for a tavern, a store, & I should imagine hog's pen stable & every thing else– The air is so impure I have scarcely been able to swallow since I enter'd the house– The land-lady is a fat, dirty, ugly looking creature, yet I must confess very obliging– She has a very suspicious coun-tenance & I am very afraid of her– She seems to be master, as well as mistress & storekeeper, & from the great noise she has been making directly under me for this half hour, I suspect she has been "stoning the raisins & watering the rum"– All the evening there has been a store full of noisy drunken fellows, yet Mr Wolcott could not be persuaded to bring in

[5]

but a small part of the baggage, & has left it in the waggon before the door, as handy as possible– Miss W's trunk is in the bar-room unlock'd the key being broken today– it contains a bag of money of her father's, yet she could not persuade him to bring it up stairs–– I feel so uneasy I cannot sleep & had therefore rather write than not this hour– some one has just gone below stairs after being as I suppos'd in bed this some time– for what purpose I know not– unless to go to our trunks or waggon– the old woman, (for it was her who went down,) tells me I must put out my candle so good night–––– Tuesday Morn–– I went to bed last night with fear & trembling, & feel truly glad to wake up & find myself alive & well– if our property is all safe, we shall have double cause to be thankful–– The old woman kept walking about after I was in bed, & I then heard her in close confab with her husband a long time–– Our room is just large enough to contain a bed a chair & a very small stand– our bed has one brown sheet & one pillow– the sheet however appear'd to be clean, which was more than we got at Nash's– there we were all oblig'd to sleep in the same room without curtains or any other screen– & our sheets there were so dirty I felt afraid to sleep in them– We were not much in favor at our first arrival there; but before we left them, they appear'd quite to like us– & I don't know why they should not, for we were all very clever, notwith-standing we rode in a waggon–– Mrs Nash said she should reckon on't to see us again (Miss W & me) so I told her that in 3 years she might expect to see me–

She said I should never come back alone, that I would
certainly be married in a little while– but I am now
more than ever determin'd not to oblige myself to
spend my days there, by marrying should I even have
an opporty—   I am oblig'd to write every way so
you must not wonder at the badness of the writing– I
am now in bed & writing in my lap– Susan has gone
to see if our baggage is in order—   I hear the old
woman's voice talking to the good deacon– & an "I
beg your pardon" comes out at every breath almost— Oh I cannot bear to see her again she is
such a disgusting object—   The men have been
swearing & laughing in the store under me this
hour– & the air of my room is so intolerable, that I
must quit my writing to go in search of some that
is *breathable*– I don't know how far I shall be
oblig'd to go for it– but there is none very near I
am certain—   Having a few moments more to
spare before we set out, with my book still in my
lap, I hasten to tell you we found everything perfectly safe, & I believe I wrong'd them all by sus-
picions— The house by day light looks worse then
ever– every kind of thing in the room where they
live– a chicken half pick'd hangs over the door– &
pots, kettles, dirty dishes, potatoe barrels– & every
thing else– & the old woman– it is beyond my power
to describe her– but she & her husband & both very
kind & obliging– it is as much as a body's life is
worth to go near them— The air has already had a
medicinal effect upon me— I feel as if I had taken
an emetic– & should stay till night I most certainly

should be oblig'd to take my bed, & that would be certain death— I did not think I could eat in the house– but I did not dare refuse– the good deacon nor his wife did not mind it, so I thought I must not— The old creature sits by eating, & we are just going to my great joy so good bye, good bye till to night——

Tuesday Noon– Ferry House near
State Prison–

It has been very cold & dusty riding to day— We have met with no adventure yet, of any kind— We are now waiting at the ferry house to cross the river as soon as wind & tide serve– The white waves foam terribly how we shall get across I know not, but I am in great fear– If we drown there will be an end of my journal——

Hobuck, Wednesday Morn–
Buskirck's Inn—

After waiting 3 or 4 hours at the ferry house, we with great difficulty cross'd the ferry & I, standing brac'd against one side of the boat involuntarily endeavouring to balance it with my weight & groaning at every fresh breeze as I watch'd the side which almost dipt in the water– & the ferrymen swearing at every breath– M^r, M^rs & Miss Wolcott viewing the city and vainly wishing they had improv'd the time of our delay to take a nearer view—— At length we reach'd this shore almost frozen– The

Ferry is a mile & an half wide– – I was too fatigued
to write last night & soon after we came retired to
bed– We were again oblig'd all to sleep in one room
& in dirty sheets– but pass'd the night very comfortably–– If good wishes have any influence, we shall
reach our journey's end in peace– for we obtain them
from everyone–– The morning is pleasant & we are
soon to ride–––– Mrs Buskirck the landlady, I should
imagine is about 60 years of age & she sits by with
a three year old child in her lap– She wears a long
ear'd cap & looks so old I thought she must be
Grandmother till I enquir'd––

Springfield–New Jersey– Pierson's Inn–

Wedy–PM 4 oclock–

"What is every body's business is no body's" for
instance– it is nobody's business where we are going,
yet every body enquires– every toll gatherer & child
that sees us–––– I am almost discouraged– we shall
never get to New Connecticut or any where else, at
the rate we go on– We went but eleven miles yesterday & 15 to day–– Our Waggon wants repairing &
we were oblig'd to put up for the night at about 3
oclock.–––– I think the country so far, much pleasanter than any part of Connecticut we pass'd thro'–
but the Turnpike roads are not half as good– The
Deacon & his family complain most bitterly of the
gates & toll bridges– tho' the former is very good-
natur'd with his complaints–– Also the tavern expenses are a great trouble– As I said before I will
never go with a Deacon again– for we go so slow &

[9]

so cheap, that I am almost tir'd to death. The horses walk, walk hour after hour while M^r W sits *reckoning his expenses* & forgetting to drive till some of us ask when we shall get there?– then he remembers the longer we are on the road the more *expensive* it will be, & whips up his horses—and when Erastus the son, drives, we go still slower for fear of hurting the horses— Since I left you I have conceived such an aversion for Doctors & the words, expense, expensive, cheap & expect, that I do not desire ever to see the one (at least to need them) or hear the others again, in my life— I have just found out that Elizabeth Town is but 5 miles off & have been to the landlord to enquire if I cannot possibly get there & he encourages me a little, I cannot write more till I am certain– Oh if I can but see my brother! After a long crying spell, I once more take up my pen to tell you I cannot go,– there is no chair or side saddle to be got, & I will, by supposing him at New York, try to content myself– to describe my disappointment would be impossible—it is such an agravation of my pain, to know myself so near & then not see him— I have the greater part of the time till now, felt in better spirits than I expected– my journal has been of use to me in that respect——— I did not know but I should meet with the same fate that a cousin of Mr Hall's did, who like me, was journeying to a new, if not a western country– She was married on her way & prevented from proceeding to her journey's end– There was a man to day in Camptown where we stopt to eat, not oats but

gingerbread, who enquired, or rather *expected* we were going to the Hio— we told him yes & he at once concluded it was to get husbands— He said winter was coming on & he wanted a wife & believ'd he must go there to get him one— I concluded of course the next thing would be, a proposal to Miss W or me to stay behind to save trouble for us both; but nothing would suit him but a rich widow, so our hopes were soon at an end— Disappointment is the lot of man & we may as well bear them with a good grace– this thought restrain'd my tears at that time, but has not been able to since— What shall I do? My companions say they shall insist upon seeing my journal & I certainly will not show it to them, so I told them I would bring it with me the first time I came to Henshaw (the place where they live) & read it to them; but I shall do my utmost to send it to you before I go– that would be a sufficient excuse for not performing my promise which must be conditional— I will not insist upon your reading this thro' my dear Elizabeth & I suspect by this time you feel quite willing to leave it unread further– I wish I could make it more interesting— I write just as I feel & think at the moment & I feel as much in haste to write every thing that occurs, as if you could know it the moment it was written– I must now leave you to write to my brother, for if I cannot see him I will at least write him– I cannot bear the idea of leaving the state without once more seeing him— I hope next to write you from 30 miles hence at least–
–Poor Susan feels worse to night than me, & M^{rs}

Wolcott to cheer us, tells us what we have yet to
expect– this you may be sure has the desir'd effect &
raises our spirits at once—

Friday morn– Chester N J.

We left Springfield yesterday about nine oclock &
came on to Chester about 22 miles from Spring^{d}——
Patience & perseverance will get us to N C in time–
but I fear we shall winter on our way there, for
instead of four weeks, I fear we shall be four times
four—— We found an excellent tavern here compar'd with any we have yet found, & we had for the
first time clean sheets to sleep in–   We pass'd thro'
Morristown yesterday, & 3. small villages– one
called Chatham I do not know the names of the
others— It is very hilly in N Jersey, & what is very
strange, we appear almost always to be going up hill,
but like the squirrel, never rise 2 inches higher– The
hills look very handsomely at a little distance,– but
none of them are very high—— M^{r} & Mrs Wolcott,
after telling us every thing dreadful, they could think
of, began encouraging us by changing sides & relating
the good as well as the bad– They are sure I shall
like Warren better than I expect & think I shall
not regret going in the least—— The weather yesterday was very pleasant, & is this morning also– We
wish to reach Easton to day, but I am sure we shall
not, for it is 32 miles distant– 5 or 600 hundred miles
appears like a short journey to me now– indeed I
feel as if I could go almost any distance– My cour-
age & spirits & both very good—one week is already

gone of the 4— I wish I could fly back to you a few minutes while we are waiting——

Mansfield–N J–Sat–morn October 27–

We yesterday travell'd the worst road you can imagine– over mountains & thro' vallies– We have not I believe, had 20 rods of level ground the whole day– and the road some part of it so intolerably bad on every account, so rocky & so gullied, as to be almost impassable– 15 miles this side Morristown, we cross'd a mountain call'd Schyler or something like it– We walk'd up it, & M^{rs} W told us it was a little like some of the mountains only not half so bad—indeed every difficulty we meet with is compar'd to something worse that we have yet to expect– We found a house built in the heart of the mountain near some springs– in a romantic place– Whether the springs are medicinal or not, I do not know– but I suspect they are, & that the house is built for the accommodation of those who go to them– for no human creature, I am sure, would wish to live there– Opposite the house are stairs on the side of the mountain & a small house resembling a bathing house, at the head of them— Soon after we cross'd the mountain, we took a wrong road, owing to the neglect of those whose duty it is to erect guide boards, & to some awkward directions given-– This gave us a great deal of trouble, for we were oblig'd in order to get right again, to go across a field where the stones were so large & so thick that we scarcely touch'd the ground the whole distance– At last the

[13]

road seem'd to end in a hogs pen, but we found it
possible to get round it, & once more found ourselves
right again–   We met very few people, yet the road
seem'd to have been a great deal travelled– One
young man came along & caus'd us some diversion,
for he eyed us very closely & then enter'd into conversation with M^r W who was walking a little forward– He told him he should himself set out next
week for Pittsburg– & we expect to see him again
before we get there— Erastus enquir'd the road of
him & he said we must go the same way he did; so
we follow'd on till we put up for the night; he walking his horse all the way & looking back at the waggon– As soon as we came to the inn he sat on his
horse at the door till he saw us all quietly seated in
the house & then rode off– Which of us made a con-
quest I know not, but I am sure one of us did— –We
have pass'd thro' but 2 towns in N J– but several
small villages– Dutch valley, between some high hills
& the Mountain– Batestown, where we stopt to *bait*–
& some others– all too small to deserve a name– At
last we stopt at Mansfield at an Inn kept by Philip
fits (a little f). We found it kept by 2 young
women, whom I thought *amazoons*– for they swore
& flew about "like *witches*"   they talk & laugh'd
about their sparks &c &c till it made us laugh so as
almost to affront them– There was a young woman
visiting them who reminded me of Lady Di Spanker–
for sprung from the ground to her horse with as
much agility as that Lady could have done— They
all took their pipes before tea– – one of them ap-

pears to be very unhappy– I believe she has a very cross husband if she is married– She has a baby & a pretty one–– Their manner̃s soften'd down after a while & the appear to be obliging & good natur'd––––

Pennsylvania– Saturday eve– 2 miles
from Bethlehem– Hanover– Oct 27th

Before I write you anything I will tell you where & how we are– We are at a dutch tavern almost crazy– In one corner of the room are a set of dutchmen talking singin & laughing in dutch so loud, that my brain is almost turn'd– they one moment catch up a fiddle & I expect soon to be pulled up to dance– I am so afraid of them I dare hardly stay in the house one night; much less over the sabbath– I cannot write so good night––

Sunday Morn--

I have hesitated a long time whether I ought to write or not, & have at length concluded I may as well write as anything else, for I cannot read or listen to Deacon W who is reading– for I am almost distracted. We have determin'd (or rather Mr W has & we must do as he says) to spend the Sabbath among these wicked wretches– It would not be against my conscience to ride to day rather than stay here, for we can do no good & get none– & how much harm they may do us I know not– but they look as if they had sufficient inclination to do us evil––

A JOURNEY TO OHIO

Sunday eve– Sundown–

I can wait no longer to write you, for I have a
great deal to say– I should not have thought it possible to pass a Sabbath in our country among such a
dissolute vicious set of wretches as we are now
among—I believe at least 50 dutchmen have been
here to day to smoke, drink, swear, pitch cents,
almost dance, laugh & talk dutch & stare at us– They
come in, in droves young & old– black & white– wom-
en & children– It is dreadful to see so many people
that you cannot speak to or understand— They are
all high dutch, but I hope not a true specimen of the
Pennsylvanians generally— Just as we set down to
tea, in came a dozen or two of women, each with a
child in her arms, & stood round the room– I did not
know but they had come in a body to claim me as one
of their kin, for they all resemble me– but as they
said nothing to me, I concluded they came to see us
Yankees, as they would a learned pig— The
women dress in striped linsey woolsey petticoats &
short gowns not 6 inches in length– they look very
strangely– The men dress much better– they put on
their best cloaths on sunday, which I suppose is their
only holiday, & "keep it up" as they call it— A
stage came on from Bethlehem & stopt here, with 2
girls & a well dress'd *fellow* who sat between them
an arm round each— They were probably going to
the next town to a dance or a frolic of some kind–
for the driver, who was very familiar with them, said
he felt just right for a frolic— I suspect more liquor

[16]

has been sold to day than all the week besides— The children have been calling us Yankees (which is the only english word they can speak) all day long– Whether it was meant as a term of derision or not, I neither know nor care– of this I am sure, they cannot feel more contempt for me than I do for them;–tho' I most sincerely pity their ignorance & folly– There seems to be no hope of their improvement as they will not attend to any means–　After saying so much about the people, I will describe our yester-day's ride– but first I will describe our last nights lodging– Susan & me ask'd to go to bed– & Mrs W spoke to Mr Riker the landlord–(for no woman was visible)– So he took up a candle to light us & we ask'd Mrs W to go up with us, for we did not dare go alone– when we got into a room he went to the bed & open'd it for us, while we were almost dying with laughter, & then stood waiting with the candle for us to get into bed– but Mrs W– as soon as she could speak, told him she would wait & bring down the candle & he then left us– I never laugh'd so heart-ily in my life– Our bed to sleep on was straw, & then a feather bed for covering– The pillows contain'd nearly a single handful of feathers, & were cover'd with the most curious & dirty patchwork, I ever saw– We had one bedquilt & one sheet– I did not undress at all, for I expected dutchmen in every moment & you may suppose slept very comfortably in that ex-pectation– – Mr & Mrs W, & another woman slept in the same room– When the latter came to bed, the man came in & open'd her bed also, after we were all in bed in the middle of the night, I was awaken'd by the entrance of three dutchmen, who were in search of a bed– I was almost frightened to death– but Mr W at length heard & stopt them before they had quite reach'd our bed– Before we were dress'd the men were at the door– which could not fasten, looking at us– I think *wild Indians* will be less terrible to me, than these creatures– Nothing vexes me more than to see them set & look at us & talk in dutch and laugh— Now for our ride– After we left Mansfield, we cross'd the longest hills, and the worst road, I ever saw– two or three times after riding a little distance on turnpike, we found it fenced across & were oblig'd to turn into a wood where it was almost impossible to proceed– large trees were across, not the road for there was none, but the only place we could possibly ride– It appear'd to me, we had come to an end of the habitable part of the globe– but all these difficulties were at last surmounted, & we reach'd the Delaware– The river where it is cross'd, is much smaller than I suppos'd– The bridge over it is elegant I think— It is covered & has 16 windows each side— As soon as we pass'd the bridge, we enter'd Easton, the first town in Pennsylvania– It is a small but pleasant town– the houses are chiefly small, & built of stone– very near together– The meeting house, Bank, & I think, market, are all of the same description– There are a few very handsome brick houses, & some wooden buildings— From Easton, we came to Bethlehem, which is 12 miles distant from it– Mr W. went a mile out of his

way, that we might see the town– It contains almost
entirely dutch people–– The houses there are nearly
all stone– but like Easton it contains some pretty
brick houses– It has not half as many stores as
Easton– –   The meeting house is a curious building– it looks like a castle– I suppose it is stone,– the
outside is plaister'd– We left our waggon to view
the town– we did not know whether the building was
a church or the moravian school, so we enquir'd of
2 or 3 men who only answer'd in dutch– Mr & Mrs
W were purchasing bread, & Susan & I walk'd on to
enquire– we next saw a little boy on horseback, & he
could only say "me cannot english" but he I believe,
spoke to another, for a very pretty boy came near
us & bow'd & expecting us to speak, which we soon
did; & he pointed out the school & explained the
different buildings to us as well as he was able; but
we found it difficult to understand him, for he could
but just "english"– We felt very much oblig'd to him,
though we neglected to tell him so– He is the only
polite dutchman small or great, we have yet seen;
& I am unwilling to suppose him a *dutchman*.   The
school buildings are low, long stone houses– the stone
houses are not at all handsome– but rather ugly––
Where we stopt to bait yesterday, we found another
waggon containing a widow Jackson, her 2 sons &
a daughter in law– They enquir'd where we going
& told us they were going to the same place & immediately join'd our party– We were sorry as we did
not wish an addition to our party, & thought by not
travvelling on sunday we should lose their company,

[19]

but rather than lose ours, they wait till monday–
They are very clever people apparently, & we may
possibly be benefited by them before we end our
journey——We now find the benefit of having our own
provision– for I would not eat anything we could get
here.

Monday morn–October 29–

It rains & we shall have a dismal day I am afraid–
M^r W's harness last night was very much injur'd by
being chew'd to pieces by a cow– I have broken my
parasol handle a little, but it will not much injure it–
I have a bad cold to day– which I know not how I
have taken– I more than ever wish to reach Warren——

Pennsylvania– Monday–eve– A Dutchman's
inn– I dont know where. Palks County–
or some thing like it——

We have only pass'd thro' 2 small towns to day,
Allenstown & Kluztown– The former is about 3
miles from Hannover, where we spent the sabbath,
& 6 from Bethlehem– Before we enter'd the town,
we cross'd the Lehi in 2 places– It was not deep, &
we forded it to save time & *expence*– It runs I believe
through Bethlehem or at the side of it & is a very
small river– Allenstown is not a pleasant place–
The houses are almost all stone– It contains 2 small
stone churches– We went into a store, where I
bought me a coarse tooth comb for 15 cents– I should
never get accustom'd to the Pensylvania currency–

A JOURNEY TO OHIO

It diverts me to hear them talk of their fippenny bits (as they pronounce it) & their eleven penny bits— Kluztown is but a few miles from Allentown– It has but one short street which is very thickly built with Stone & log houses— It is rather a dirty street & not more pleasant than the others Stone is used for everything in this state– The barns & houses are almost entirely built of it– I imagine the dutch pride themselves on building good barns, for a great many of them are very elegant– they are 3 & 4 stories high, have windows & one or 2. I saw with blinds– They are larger & handsomer than most of the houses– The dutch women are all out as we pass, dressing flax, picking up apples &c &c– The dress of the women grows worse & worse– We find them now with very short petticoats, no short gown & barefoot— The country is not pleasant, at least does not appear so as we ride thro' it at all– I should think the land must be good as we see large fields of grain very frequently– There does not appear to be as much fruit as in N Y & N J— We saw immense quantities of apples in each of those states, particularly N J– there would be thousands of bushels at the cider presses, & still the trees would be borne down with them— The roads in this state are pretty good, where, dame Nature has not undertaken to pave them– but she has so much other business on hand that she has never learn'd to pave, & makes a wretched hand at it– I wish she could be persuaded to leave it to Art for the future; for we are very great sufferers for her work– It is quite amusing to see the variety of paintings on the inn-keeper's signs– I saw one in N J with Thos Jeff'ns head & shoulders & his name above it– to day I saw Gen G Washington– his name underneath– Gen Putnam riding down the steps at Horseneck– one sign was merely 3 little kegs hanging down one after the other– They have the sun rising, setting, & at Meridian, here a full moon, a new moon, the moon & 7 stars around her, the Lion & Unicorn "fighting &c", & every thing else that a dutchman has ever seen or heard of– I do not believe one of them has wit enough to invent any thing, even for a sign——— Several of these creatures sit by Jabbering dutch so fast, that my brain is turn'd & my thoughts distracted, & I wonder I have been able to write a word– If you find it unintelligible you must not wonder or blame me– A dozen will talk at once & it is really intolerable– I wish Uncle Porter was here– How can I live among them 3 weeks?   We have come about 24 miles to day– it rain'd a very little this morning & the rest of the day has been quite pleasant tho' somewhat cold– Tomorrow we pass thro' Reading—

Wednesday Octber 31st Highdleburg–Penn–

We pass'd through Reading yesterday which is one of the largest & prettiest towns I have seen– We stopt about 2 hours in the town, & I improved my time in walking about to see it– I went into the stores enquiring for a scissor case– Almost every one could talk english– but I believe the greatest part of them were dutch people– As soon as we left Reading, we cross'd the Schuylkill– It was not deeper than the Lehi, & we rode thro' it in our waggon. A bridge was begun over it, but the man broke & was unable to finish it– It would have been an excellent one had it been completed– It is now grown over with grass & serves as a walk for the ladies– – We put up for the night at Leonard Shaver's tavern– He is a dutchman, but has one of the most agreeable women for his wife I have seen in this State– I was extremely tir'd when we stopt, & went immediately to bed after tea– & for the first time for a long while, undress'd me & had a comfortable nights rest– We are oblig'd to sleep every & any way– at most of the inns now– – My companions were all disturb'd by the waggoners who put up here & were all night in the room below us, eating, drinking, talking, laughing & swearing– Poor Mr W– was so disturb'd that he is not well this morning, & what is more unpleasant to us, is not good natur'd, & Mrs W has been urging him this half hour, to eat some breakfast– he would only answer "I shan't eat any"– but at length swallow'd some in sullen silence– but is in a different way preparing to ride–— If I were going to be married I would give my *intended,* a gentle emetic, or some such thing to see how he would bear being sick a little– for I could not coax a husband as I would a child, only because he was a little sick & a great deal cross– I trust I shall never have the trial– I am sure I should never bear it with temper & patience. Mr W is I believe a very pious good man, but not naturally pleasant temper'd– religion however, has corrected it in a great degree, but not wholly overcome it– Mrs W– is an amiable sweet temper'd woman, as I ever saw; the more I know her, the better I love her– Susan is a charming girl– but Erastus is rather an obstinate boy– he feels superiour to his father & every one else, in wisdom—Mrs Jackson is a clever woman I believe, but I have a prejudice against her which I cannot overcome– She is very inquisitive and very communicative– She resembles Moll Lyman or rather crazy Moll of Northampton in her looks– She has considerable property & feels it very sensibly– Her youngest son is almost eighteen & has his wife with him, who is not quite as old– They have been married 2 months, & are a most loving couple– I cannot help thinking whenever I see them together, of "love I Sophia?" &c— Her name is Eliza & his, John— The other son is a very obliging but not a very polish'd young man– I like them all better than at first——

Wednesday Eve– Miller's town– Penn– Oct–31st

We have come 24 miles to day, & just begin to shorten the distance between Pittsburgh & us, & to increase it between Phildelphy (as the dutchmen call it,) & us– It has for a long time been 250 miles to Pittsg & 60 to Philhia– but is now 218 to one & more than 80 to the other— It began snowing this morning which rendered our ride more unpleasant than before– Mr W has continued just as he was in the morning– scarcely a word has been spoken by any of us– I never felt more low spirited & discouraged in my life– We have pass'd through 2 little towns to day– Moyerstown & the other I don't know the name of– We also pass'd thro Lebanon which appear'd to be a town of considerable size & pleasant– we did not stop at all in it– The other towns were merely one short dirty street– this town is one street only, but a tolerably pretty one– There are a number of good houses in it– We have once more got among people of our own nation & language– & they appear very clever– –

Harrisburg– P– Thursday– Eve–
November–1st 1810–

It has been snowing fast all the afternoon & we found it very difficult travelling & were oblig'd to put up just in the edge of the town– It was Mr W's intention to cross the Susquehannah which is the other side the town– we shall not pass thro' it– We cross'd the Sweet Arrow, a little river about 8 miles from the Susquehannah– we cross'd it in our waggon– Mr Jeremiah Rees is our landlord– his wife is sick with a fever arising from the Hives at first– He has a sister who seems to take the direction of the female part of the business– She is a strange creature–

Friday morn– I have been very much diverted at hearing some part of her history which she told last night, after drinking a little too much I suppose– She says she has property if she is not married– she had her fortune told a short time since– & was told to

[25]

think of a certain gentleman living about 300 miles off– which she did, & thought so hard that a drop of blood fell from her nose– She was telling Mrs Jackson of this & ask'd how far she was going– being told about 300 miles– well she said she really believ'd her oldest son was the young man she was to have, for he looks just like the one she thought of– The young man will be quite flatter'd no doubt—— We are all in tolerably good spirits notwithstanding we are unable to proceed on our journey—   It still continues snowing, & we shall stay here till tomorrow morning & how much longer I do not know– – There was a cockfighting in the house last night & a great many of the "finest young men in the town" got so intoxicated as to be unable to get home without assistance—— M. V. D.

Sunday eve– East pensboro' township– P–

We left Mr Rees' yesterday ten oclock– & after waiting some time at the ferry house, cross'd the Susquehanna with considerable difficulty– The river is a mile wide & so shallow that the boat would scrape across the large stones so as almost to prevent it from proceeding– We only came 8 miles– the riding was awful– & the weather so cold that I thought I should perish riding 4 miles– This will do well for us, 8 miles in 3 days– We were to have seen the mountains yesterday, but are 50 miles from it—   I should like to have staid at Mr Rees' till we reach home if it was possible, notwithstanding we had like to have all lost our characters there– While we were at breakfast, the black wench miss'd nearly 4 dollars of money, & very impudently accused us with taking it, in rather an indirect manner— I felt at first very angry, but anger soon gave place to pity for the poor girls loss– It was money she had been saving for a long time that she might get enough to buy her a dress– but she left it about very carelessly in the closet where any one might have taken it who was so disposed— But had I been inclined to steal, I could not have stolen from a poor black girl– I would rather have given her as much– I never felt so queerly in my life– To be suspected of theft was so new & unexpected to me, that I was wholly unprepar'd for it— We went to Mr Rees & begg'd him to take some method to satisfy the girl we were innocent but we could not prevail on him to, tho' we really wish'd it– He gave the girl a severe scolding & desir'd us not to remember it against them, or to suffer ourselves to be made a moment uneasy by it, & both himself and Mrs Rees were extremely sorry any thing of the kind had happen'd– The girl continued crying & assuring us her money had been safe all summer till then & nobody had been near it but us– I, nor any of us had any doubt that the landlord's sister, whom I before mention'd, had taken it– She had the day before 2 or 3 ninepences in her shoes, & when M^r W ventur'd to ask her if she had not taken it to tease the wench, she swore by every thing she had not touch'd it– She said it was fashionable for ladies to carry money in their shoes– I suppose she had long been eyeing it, & thought then would be a good opperty to take it but did not intend it should be discover'd till we were gone & unable to defend ourselves from the charge which she then meant to make against us— She is so worthless a character in every respect, that I am certain she could be guilty of stealing upon occasion— She was very fond of telling what ladies, like *her* & *me,* did & wore— She is between 30 & 40 yrs of age– It was an honour I was not very tenacious of, to be rank'd with her ladyship– The money was not found before we left there & I suppose the poor girl feels as certain some one of us have it, as that she has lost it– Should I ever return this way I would call & enquire about it– I hope it will be found with Babby (for that is the creatures name)—

We put up for the Sabbath at a tavern where none but the servants deign to look at us– When I am with such people, my proud spirit rises & I feel superior to them all— I believe no regard is paid to the sabbath any where in this State– It is only made a holiday of— So much swearing as I have heard amongst the Pensylvanians both men & women I have never heard before during my whole life– I feel afraid I shall become so accustom'd to hearing it, as to feel no uneasiness at it.   Harrisburgh is a most dissipated place I am sure– & the small towns seem to partake of the vice & dissipation of the great ones— I believe Mrs Jackson has cast her eyes on Susan or me for a daughter in law– for my part, though I feel very well disposed toward the young man, I had not thought of *making a bargain* with him, but I have jolted off most of my high notions, & perhaps I may be willing to descend from a judge to a blacksmith– I shall not absolutely determine with respect to him till I get to Warren & have time to look about me & compare him with the judges Dobson & Stephenson– It is clever to have two or three strings to ones bow— But in spite of my prejudices, they are *very clever*— Among my list of *cast offs,* I would rank Dutchmen, a Pensylvania waggoner, ditto gentlemen– for their prophanity– & a Slut– The words, Landlord & lady, terrible,– get married,– get a husband–&c &c— I do not find it as easy to write a journal as I had hoped– for we are seldom favour'd with any more than the barroom, & there is always as many men as the room will hold besides our party, & there is nine of us– so you may judge whether I find it difficult or not– I frequently begin a sentence & forget how to finish it,– for the conversation grows so loud, that I am oblig'd to listen to it & write between whiles– I sometimes get quite discouraged & think I will not try again, but I take too much pleasure in writing, to give it up willingly—

10 miles West of Carlisle– Penn–
Monday Nov–5th–

We came but a little peice as the Dutchmen say, to day, & are in a most curious place to night– If possible I will describe it– It is a log hut built across the road from the tavern, for *movers*– that the land-

[29]

lord need not be *bother'd* with them— Had it been
possible for our horses to have reached another inn
we should not have staid with the cross old dutch fellow– we have a good fire, a long dirty table, a few
boards nailed up for a closet, a dozen long boards in
one side & as many barrels in the other– 2 benches to
sit on, two bottomless chairs, & a floor containing dirt
enough to plant potatoes— The man says he has
been so bother'd with movers, that he has taken
down his sign, for he does not need his tavern to
live— If we had a mind to stay we might but if we
chose to go on he had no objection— Cross old
witch– I had rather have walk'd 10 miles than stay,
but the poor horses could not— We are going to
sleep on the floor all in a room together in the old
stile without bothering the old Scamp, for any thing–
Mrs Jackson has beds— If I did not feel provok'd
with the wretch I should rest comfortably–

Tues– morn– The old man I believe feels a little
asham'd of his treatment of us & was going to make
some apology, but concluded by saying with a forced
laugh, that if we ever came there again, he would
treat us just so– He may if has opporty—

Tuesday night– Nov–6th–

We have only counted 17 miles to day although
the riding has been much better than for several
days past– We stopt in Shippenburgh at noon– The
town contains only one street a mile & a half in
length & very thickly built– The street is some part
of it pleasant, & some part dirty— I saw in it a

handsome young gentleman who was both a dutchman & Pennsylvanian, yet in an hour & half I did
not hear him make use of a single oath or prophane
word– It was a remarkable instance, the only one I
have known, & I could not but remark it– Prophanity
is the characteristic of a Pennsylvanian– — We are 4
miles from Strasburgh & the mountains, & one of
our horses is ill, owing to Erastus giving him too
many oats– Erastus is master rather than his father,
& will do as he pleases for all any one– He is a stub-
born fellow, & so impudent to his mother & sister,
that I have no patience with him– – We are not as
bless'd as the Israelites were, for our shoes wax old
& our cloaths wear out– – I don't know that mine will
last till I get there——— —— —— ——— —— ——

Wed– morn– Last night Susan & I went to bed
early, as we slept ill the night before– we expected to
get good beds & were never so disappointed– We
were put in an old garret that had holes in the roof
big enough to crawl through– Our bed was on the
floor, harder it appear'd to me, than boards could
be– & dirty as possible– a dirty feather bed our only
covering– After lying an hour or two, we complain'd to Mrs Wolcott who applied to the landlady
for a bedstead, but could only obtain leave for us
to sleep on one bed with another over us– I slept
wretchedly & feel very little like climbing a mountain— Mr & Mrs W could not sleep at all & got up
at about eleven oclock— She had good beds in the
house or I would not have complained so much—

[31]

A JOURNEY TO OHIO

Jennyauter–P—Wednesday 2 oclock P M–

between 2 brothers——

This morning we cross'd the first mountain call'd first brother, & are in an inn between the first & second brother; the latter we are soon to ascend– The first m-n is 3 1-2 miles over,– better road than we expected– but bad enough to tire the horses almost to death– We met & were overtaken by a number of people— We all walk'd the whole distance over– I did not stop at all to rest till I reach'd the top– I was then oblig'd to wait for some of them to overtake me, as I had outwalk'd them all. It is not a little fatiguing to walk up a long mountain I find— When we had nearly reach'd the foot of it, we heard some music in the valey below, & not one of us could imagine from what it proceeded; but soon found it was from the bells of a waggoner– He had twelve bells on the collars of his horses, (not sleigh bells) & they made a great variety of sounds which were really musical at a distance— We found at the tavern where we are now, or rather they came after us, a Mr Beach, & his wife who was confin'd nine days after she set out on her journey, with a little son– It is just a fortnight since she was confin'd, & this morning she ventur'd to set out on her journey again– They came from Morristown– N J– & are going to some part of the Ohio, much farther than we are going. Mrs B– appears to be a very pretty woman & quite a lady– Her father & mother, a sister & 3 little children, set out with them, but were oblig'd to leave them & go on, as soon as Mrs B was confin'd– I feel afraid she will catch her death, tho' every care is taken to render her journey safe & comfortable–– She & babe are both very well now––

Fannitsburg– Penn– McAllen's Inn–
Wednesday night– Nov– 6th–

We have over come 2 mountains to day– & are between the 2d & 3d brothers– We walked over it– I have walked about 8 miles to day & feel as much fatigued as I have almost ever been in my life– It was 4 *long* miles over– We met a number of wag-gons on it– but no other travellers– This is a very small but pretty place– The 3 first m-ns are very near each other– the 4th is 40 or 50 miles distant–– They are higher than I expected, & make a formid-able appearance– It has been very smoky all day– I am so tir'd I can neither think or write, so good night––––

Thursday morn– We had a good nights rest, but I am so lame I can scarcely walk this morning– I have a mountain to walk over, notwithstanding–– Mr W's horses grow so dull that he expects to be oblig'd to put up for a few days, & we are all almost dis-couraged–– The weather looks stormy & where we shall get to or what we shall do, I cannot imagine–– The Jacksons enquire about the road & the moun-tains &c &c, of every one they see, & get such dif-ferent & contradictory answers from each one, that

[33]

it perplexes & discourages us all– I wish they would be contented to wait patiently till time & experience inform them what they cannot find out any other way– Mr W says I have now an opporty to experience the truth of a text of scripture which says "all men are liars"– I found that out long ago– & this journey confirms the truth of it.

Peach Orchard, P– Thursday night–
Phelps' Tavern—

I do not feel to night, my dear Elizabeth, as if I should ever see you again– 3 mountains & more hundreds of miles part us; & tho' I cannot give up the idea of returning, I cannot think of traversing this road again– If I live to return I will wait till the new turnpike is finished— We cross'd the last brother this morning, & found the greater part of it, better than the other two– but about 60 rods near the top it was excessively steep— We found a house at the foot of the steepest part– A woman & her 2 sons live there & keep cakes & beer— The woman told us she had no husband at *present*—I suppose she has one in expectation—On the first mountain, I found some sweet Williams— We stopt at noon, at a dismal looking log hut tavern– The landlady (I hate the word but I must use it,) talk'd about bigotry, bigotted notions, liberty of conscience &c– She did not look as if she knew the meaning of conscience, much less of bigotry— All this afternoon we have been walking over young mountains, distant relations of

the 3 brothers, but not half as clever– I was so lame
& so tir'd that for an hour I did not know but I must
set down & die– I could not ride– the road was so
bad, it was worse than walking– I would not tell you
all this, if you were to receive this before it is all
over– – It rain'd a very little all day, but just at night
it began to rain very fast, & I expected we should all
catch our death, walking thro' mud & mire, with no
umbrella, or but one that would not cover us all – We
were wet thro before we reach'd this dreadful place
where we now are–– The Woman is cross & the
Man sick– ––

Friday night– It rain'd all day yesterday, & such a
shocking place as this is, I never saw– A dozen Waggoners are here, some half drunk & no place for us
to stay in but our waggons or a little chamber with 3
squares of glass in it– with scarcely room to sit or
stand––

Saturday morn– – I am now in despair, it continues raining faster than ever– The house full
of drunken prophane wretches, the old woman cross
as a witch– We have nothing to eat & can get nothing but some slapjacks at a baker's some distance off,
& so stormy we cannot get there–– Mrs Jackson
frets all the time, I wish they would go on & leave
us, we should do as well again–– Mr Beach & his
wife & child & the woman who is with them, are
here, & the house is full– Mrs Beach rode in all the
rain Thursday, but took no cold & bears it well as
any one– It rains most dreadfully & they say it is the
clearing off shower– Oh, if it only proves so–– "Oh

had I the wings of a dove, how soon would I meet you again"– We have never found the wretches indelicate till last evening, but while we were at tea, they began talking & singing in a most dreadful manner– – We are 4 miles from Sidling hill, the next mountain, & a mile & a half from this, there is a creek which we must cross, that is so rais'd by the rain, as to render it impossible to pass it——

Saturday night– Our "clearing up shower" has lasted all day with unabated violence,— Just at sunset we had a pretty hard thunder shower, & at dusk there was clear sky visible & the evening star shone bright as possible, but now it is raining fast again— After giving an emetic I would take a long journey with my *intended,* to try his patience– – mine is try'd sorely now– I wish you could just take a peep at me– my frock is wet & dirty a quarter of a yard high, only walking about the house– I have been in my chamber almost the whole day, but was oblig'd to go down just at night to eat, & look at the sky– I was very much frighten'd by a drunken waggoner, who came up to me as I stood by the door waiting for a candle, he put his arm round my neck, & said something which I was too frighten'd to hear– It is the first time the least insult has been offer'd to any of us– One waggoner very civilly offer'd to take Susan or me, on to Pittsᵍ in his waggon if we were not like to get there till spring– It is not yet determin'd which shall go with him— One waggon in crossing the creek this afternoon, got turn'd over & very much injur'd— We have concluded the reason so few are willing to return from the Western country, is not that the country is so good, but because the journey is so bad— Mr W. has gone to & from there, 5 times, but thinks this will be the last time– Poor Susan groans & sighs & now then sheds a few tears– I think I exceed her in patience & fortitude——— Mrs Wolcott is a woman of the most perfect equanimity I ever saw– She is a woman of great feeling & tenderness, but has the most perfect command over her feelings– She is not *own* mother to these children, but she is a very good one——— I have learn'd Elizabeth, to eat raw *pork* & drink whisky– dont you think I shall do for a new country? I shall not know how to do either when I end my journey, however–   We have almost got out of the land of dutchmen, but the waggoners are worse– —— The people here talk curiously, they all reckon instead of expect–– Youns is a word I have heard used several times, but what it means I don't know, they use it so strangely— Mr Rees used to exclaim at any thing wonderful, "Only look at that now"— "I reckon you are going into the back countries" is now our usual salutation from every one––——— Susan is in bed for want of some employment & I will join her, after telling you, it has really clear'd off now, & the moon is shining in full splendor.– I hope to-morrows sun will deign to smile upon us– It is long since we have seen it– —— I expect to be oblig'd to go thro' a process of fire & brimstone at my journeys end & shall feel thankful, if that will remedy all the evils arising from dirty beds &c— I find no necessity for

even that yet, but I fear I shall soon——good
night——

Sunday 2 oclock P M– We left the Inn this morning in the hope of getting a *little piece* on our way,
but have only reach'd the baker's, half a mile from
where we set out– The creek is so high we cannot
cross it yet– An old man & his wife live here, &
appear to be very kind clever people, & what is more
than we have found before, they appear to regard
the Sabbath– They are Methodists– This is a small
log hut, but clean & comfortable– There are no waggoners here—— I shall be oblig'd to colour my frock
I believe, for it attracts the attention of those creatures so much, that I dare not go in sight of them
scarcely–   I often think of the 2 lines your Mama
repeated to us "In Silk, &c"

Sunday night.

About sunset, we left the baker's & came down to
the Creek, but found it was impossible to get over
the waggon, & the road was so intolerable between
the place we had left & the creek, that we could not
go back, & what to do, it took a long time to determine; but at length M^r W concluded we had better
come over to a dirty tavern this side, & let Erastus
sleep in the wagon—— The stream runs so fast, that
we did not dare cross it alone, as there was nothing
but a log to cross on; so the waggoners & our
own party, were oblig'd to lead & pilot us, over
the stream & thro' a most shocking place as I ever

[38]

saw– The men were all very civil– they are waiting

this line is the shape of a Pennsylvania waggon–

with their waggons, like the rest of us— — We fare
worse & worse, & still M^r W– & his wife, tell us this
is nothing to what will come– I do not fully believe
them, for we cannot endure much more & live—
Susan & young Mrs Jackson have been quite unwell
all day— I never felt in better health, & my spirits
are pretty good, considering all things— We are
not able to get beds here, & are to sleep on the floor
to night– There is another family here, with several
little children— They say there has been a *heap* of
people moving this fall;– I don't know exactly how
many a heap is, or a *sight* either, which is another
way of measuring people— I would be *apt* to think
it was a *terrible* parcel, to use the language of the
people round me—— I have such an enormous appe-
tite the whole time, that I have been in some fear of
starving– for food of every kind, is very scarce with
us– Money will not procure it, & nothing else I am
sure, will– for they love money better than life, if
possible—   4 Sabbaths we have pass'd on the
road, & I suppose 2 or 3 more will pass before we
get among people who "remember the sabbath day
to keep it holy"— We find no books to read, only at
the bakers to day I found part of a bible, a metho-
dist hymn book & a small book containing an account of the progress of Methodism throughout the
country; in letters from Ministers & others— ——
We left Mr Beach & family, at the tavern we left

to day— I hope tomorrow to write you from a comfortable place 6 or 8 miles at least from the next mountain—

Monday morn– We have now I think met with as bad as can befal us— Never, never did I pass such a night– – – We could get no bed & for a long time expected to be oblig'd to set up all night– but we could get no room nor fire to stay by, & the landlady was so kind as to give up her bed to us; so Mrs W & Susan went to bed there, while I went to bed with Mrs Jackson in another room– I took off my frock & boots, & had scarcely lain down, when one of the wretches came into the room & lay down by me on the outside of the bed– I was frighten'd almost to death & clung to Mrs Jackson who did not appear to mind it– & I lay for a quarter of an hour crying, & scolding & trembling, begging of him to leave me– At last, when persuaded I was in earnest, he begg'd of me not to take it amiss, as he intended no harm & only wish'd to become acquainted with me— A good for nothing brute, I wonder what he suppos'd I was– I don't know of any thought word or action of mine that could give him reason to suppose I would authorise such abominable insolence– – The man & his wife, who are here, & their family, John Jackson & his wife, & Mrs Jackson, were all in the room– The moment he left the room, I put on my frock & was going in to Mrs W & Susan, but I could not get to them without going thro' the room where all the waggoners were, & Mrs Jackson did not think it safe, so I got on another part of the bed where none of them could come near me, & had been there about 10 minutes when Mrs W & Susan came into the room both crying, & as much frighten'd as I had been, for one of the creatures had been into their room, & they could scarcely get him out– Mr W– was in the waggon, & the landlord was so afraid of these waggs that he did not dare stay in his own house, for they threaten'd to put him into the creek, if he did not continue giving them liquor– I wish they had put him in– a mean sneaking fellow!— His poor wife was then oblig'd to bear it all, & she was very much distress'd on our account– She was not to blame for any thing that happen'd, for as long as her husband suffer'd it, she could not prevent it– At last Mrs W– went to bed with Mrs Jackson & me, & Susan lay down with John & his wife– We lay but a few minutes, when one of them came into our room again crawling on his hands & knees– Mrs W & I sprung & run out into the mud in our stocking feet & were going to call Mr W.– but the creatures came out to us & begg'd us not to, & pledg'd their honor (of which you may suppose they possess'd a great share) that we should not be disturb'd more– & tenderness for Mr W– who we knew would be sick to day if depriv'd of rest, at length determin'd us to go back; but we did not go to bed again till just morning, when some of us slept nearly or quite an hour– which was every wink of sleep we could obtain during the whole night– The fellows were all but one, very still afterwards– Indeed there was but 2 who made any disturbance, & only one of those was very bad– but one, was a complete child of the evil one– the vilest, worst, most blasphemous wretch, that ever liv'd— Mr W– came back to the house before 2 oclock, & this morning, threaten'd them with a prosecution– They are quite angry– they are in the employ of this man who is moving; he is a merchant & they carry his goods to Pittsg—

Novbr–12th Monday night– Nail Shop–
on the 4th Mountain

We have got 8 1-2 miles on our journey to day, & now it rains again— If I could describe to you our troubles from roads, waggoners & creeks, I would,– but it is impossible— The waggoners set out just before we did & the bad one being foremost has taken all the pains in his power to hinder our progress, by driving as slow as possible & stopping every other moment– The road was too narrow to pass them, unless they would turn out for us– all but one did, but he swore he would not– We came by them as they stopp'd at noon, & put up to night at an inn on the mountain, out of the direct road, where we should peaceably pass the night– but the waggoners have follow'd us, & the house is full– They are not in our room—   Our party now consists of Mrs Jackson's, Mr Beach's & Mr W's familys— The woman who is with Mr Beach, is such a foolish old creature, that we are all out of patience with her– – She is aunt to them, I believe– — If I were to choose, I would never have company on a long journey– such company at least– Our chairs here are taken from us for the Waggoners– —— Our road over the mountains, has not even a good prospect to render it pleasant– I have been repeating to Susan all day, "Comfort damsel &c"–   Mrs Jackson is scolding because she has no chair to set on.– Mr W– tells her, "Fret not thyself because of evil doers"– – There is another impassable creek a head, & a hundred waggons waiting to cross it– Our prospect brightens fast– dont you think so?   good night—

Tuesday eve– Nov– 13th– 4 miles east of
Bedford– Penn–

We have at length escap'd the waggoners & Mr Beach– The former did not trouble us last night at all in the night– When we went to bed they watch'd us narrowly, & after we were in bed we heard them talking about us, enquiring of each other where we slept &c– We were in the room with Mr & Mrs Wolcott, directly over the room they were in, but still I felt afraid of them– The worst one is quite mad, & says he intends if possible, to give us more trouble than he has done already– The other is quite asham'd of his conduct & I suspect would be willing to make any amends in his power– He told this to Mrs Jackson who is much too familiar with them, & I believe it was owing entirely to that, that they conducted so– for the rest of us always avoid even the sight of them, as much as possible; & much more any conversation with them—— We got up very early indeed

& set out before breakfast, because the horses could have no hay, & we have got quite out of their reach— We cross'd a little stream call'd the Juniaatta– I spell the names as they are pronounced, but I do not spell them right, I am sure, nor can I find out how they are spelt many of them– The river is long & narrow– It takes a winding course thro' the mountains, & is a very pretty stream— We rode some distance on its banks, & the road been tolerable, it would have been pleasant– I have said so much about the badness of the roads that you will hardly believe me when I tell you we seen some of the worst to day we have ever found– & some, as good as any in this state– – I should not have suppos'd it possible for any thing to pass it– Mrs W said it seem'd like going into the lower regions, but I had always an idea, that road was smooth & easy– I am sure if it was as bad as that, it would have fewer travellers– We went down however till we came to a lower region– It was really awful— We saw some men to day, mending the roads– I did not think a Pennsylvanian ever touch'd a road or made a bridge, for we are oblig'd to ride thro' every stream we come to– We have been nearly 20 miles to day; & have been oblig'd to walk up hill, till we are all very tir'd– I felt too much so to write, but I am unwilling to omit it– We are now, comfortably & quietly seated, in a private house– I only wish now, we could get rid of what company we have left– but that we cannot do– – –

A JOURNEY TO OHIO

Wednesday night. A private house–
10 miles w– of Bedford

We cross'd the Juniaatta again to day, with a great deal of trouble, after waiting on its banks about 3 hours– It is astonishing how the last week's rain, rais'd every stream & overflow'd every place– The like here, has not been known for 30 years it is said— A waggoner last week, with 4 horses, was drown'd crossing a creek– He was advis'd by those who were by, not to venture– & answer'd "he would be damn'd to hell if he did not cross it"– he made the attempt & in a few minutes was sent into eternity, & probably to that awful place– — —   It has been raining very fast this afternoon, & we put up at a little log hut, a few miles west of Bedford– we came about 10 miles to day– The house is very small & there is scarcely room to move–

Thursday night– Allegany M^{tn}
Nov– 16–

We have had a warm & pleasant day till towards night, when it began to rain, as it has done every day for a fortnight– We are now at a tavern half a mile from the top of the Allegany Mt– this Mountain is 14 miles over– At the highest part of it is a most beautiful prospect of mountains– 5 or 6 ridges one after the other— We clamber'd up a high rock near to the highest part, but found the prospect little better than the one from the road– I wish I could describe it to you– We have had no prospect of any

[45]

consequence from any of the mountains before– I
have been quite disappointed at not seeing any—
We found winter green berrys in abundance on it–
I pick'd a sprig of ivy from the top, which I will
send you– call it laurel & preserve it, as it came from
the very *backbone of America,* as they all tell us—
We have walk'd a great deal to day, & indeed we are
oblig'd to every day, for the whole country seems
one continued mtn– I thought we had reach'd the top
of this, for we began to descend a little; but we have
half a mile more to ascend yet—— This house is full
of travvellers & wag'nrs but all are very peacable–
There is a curiosity in the house– a young lady who
has come from N Connecticut *unmarried*— after
staying in Warren a year—a thing I never before
heard of, & had begun to think impossible. I feel
quite encouraged by it– & do not believe the place as
dangerous as is generally reported– — I find in every
family a *Paggy*– every body is dutch— the children
& girls, are all very much attracted by my little black
buttons, & the manner in which my frock is made–
& the Wag'rs by the colour of it– There will be little
of it left by the time I get to Warren, for it is
almost gone—

Friday night– Allegany Mtn—

After a comfortable nights rest, we set out on foot
to reach the height of the mtn– It rain'd fast for a
long time, & at length began snowing– We found the
roads bad past description,– worse than you can pos-

sibly imagine– Large stones & deep mud holes every
step of the way– We were oblig'd to walk as much
as we possibly could, as the horses could scarcely stir
the waggon the mud was so deep & the stones so
large–– It has grown so cold that I fear we shall all
perish tomorrow– We suffer'd with cold excessively,
to day– From what I have seen and heard, I think
the State of Ohio will be well fill'd before winter,–
Waggons without number, every day go on– One
went on containing *forty* people– We almost every
day, see them with 18 or 20– one stopt here to night
with 21–– We are at a baker's, near a tavern which
is fill'd with movers & waggoners– It is a comfortable place, but rather small– One old man has been
in examining my writing, & giving his opinion of it
in dutch, to a young fellow who was with him– He
said he could not read a word of any thing–– He
found fault with the ink, but commended the strait-
ness & facility with which I wrote– in english– I was
glad he had not on his specs–– –– –– We came but
10 miles to day, & are yet on the Allegany– It is up
hill almost all the way down the mountains–– I do
not know when we are down them for my part––
I'm thinking as they say here, we shall be oblig'd to
winter on it, for I *reckon* we shall be unable to proceed on our journey, on account of roads, weather,
&c–– We are on the old Pennsylvania road– the
Glade road is said to be ten times worse than this–
That is utterly impossible– We thought we should
escape the waggoners this way; but find as many of
them as ever– they are a very great annoyance–– ––

What would the old man say hereto?— I am very
tir'd, so good night—

Saturday eve–2 miles from Laurel Hill–Penn–

We came but 9 or 10 miles to day, & are now near
the 6th Mountain– in a tavern fill'd with half drunken
noisy waggoners— One of them lies singing directly
before the fire; proposing just now to call for a song
from the young ladies— — —   I can neither think
nor write he makes so much noise with his *love
songs;* I am every moment expecting something
dreadful & dare not lay down my pen lest they should
think me listening to them– They are the very worst
wretches that ever liv'd, I do believe,—I am out of
all patience with them– The whole world nor any
thing in it, would tempt me to stay in this State
three months– I dislike everything belonging to it —
I am not so foolish as to suppose there are no better
people in it than those we have seen; but let them
be ever so good, I never desire to see any of them– –
We overtook an old waggoner whose waggon had
got set in the mud, & I never heard a creature swear
so– & whipt his horses till I thought they would
die — I could not but wonder at the patience and for-
bearance of the Almighty, whose awful name was so
blasphem'd—   We also overtook a young *Doctor–*
who is going with his father to Mad river in the
state of Ohio– – He has been studying physic in New
Jersey,– but appears to be an uneducated man from
the language he makes use of– —I believe both himself & his father are very clever– I heard them re-

proving a swearer— He dresses smart, & was so polite as to assist us in getting over the mud— Susan & I walk'd on before the waggon as usual, & he overtook us and invited us into the house & call'd for some brandy sling– we did not drink, which he appear'd not to like very well, & has scarcely spoken to us since– – He thinks himself a gentleman of the *first chop,* & takes the liberty of coining words for himself– Speaking of the people in this state, he said they were very ignorant & very *superstitionary*—perhaps you have heard the word before– I never did—

Sunday morn– We had good beds last night, contrary to my expectation,– and we are going on our journey this morning– It is extremely cold & very bad riding or walking– Mr W– has been so long detain'd by bad weather & riding, that he thinks himself justifiable in riding on the sabbath– I thought so some time ago—

Sunday noon– We are on the top of Laurel Hill, the 6th mountain— We women & girls, have walk'd between 5 & 6 miles this morning— We left the waggons getting along very slowly, & came on to a house to warm us– It is a log hut & full of children, as is every one we come to— The wind whistles about us, & it looks very much like snow— — One waggon got set this morning, & hinder'd us this long time— The young Doctor & his father are still in company with us— The former, who has got over his pouting fit, leaves his father to drive,– while he walks on with the ladies– he is not with us just now—

A JOURNEY TO OHIO

He has not conquer'd the antipathy I bear a young
physician– or rather a *young Doctor*– How little it
seems like the sabbath– I would not write if I could
do any thing else– but I can not even think **good**
thoughts—

Sunday eve– Nov–19th– Foot of
Laurel Hill–Penn–

I wish my dear Elizabeth, you could be here for
half an hour, & hear the strangest man talk, that
you or I ever saw in this world– He is either mad
or a fool– I don't know which, but he looking over
me & telling me I *can* make a writer– He is the most
rating, ranting fellow– I wish you could hear him—
I begin to think him mad– His name is Smith– He
& his wife are journeying either to New Orleans or
the Ohio— I never was more diverted than to hear
him (he is certainly crazy– repeating a prayer & a
sermon & forty other things in a breath) talk about
the Dutchmen in Pennsylvania– He & his wife came
amongst them one evening & stopt at several houses
to get entertainment, but was sent on by each one to
the tavern– He began by stating his religious tenets,
& at length after every body & thing was created, he
says the *under Gods* (of whom he supposes there
were a great number) took some of the skum &
stir'd it up, & those fellows came out—or rather
Hell boil'd over & they were form'd of the skum— -
I believe he has been studying all his life for hard
words & pompous speeches, & he rattled them off
at a strange rate– His language is very ungrammati-

cal– but the Jacksons are all in raptures with him—
They cannot understand his language (nor indeed
could any one else) & therefore concluded he must
be very learned– Their observations are almost as
diverting as his conversation– I could make them believe in ten minutes, that I was a girl of great larnin–
if I were to say over Kermogenious– Heterogenious
& a few such words without any connection—no
matter if I do but bring them in some how— We
are over the 6th mountain & at an Inn at the foot of
it– This mtn is called worse than any of them– it is
only about 6 miles over– We have only come 8 to
day, & I have not been in the waggon– The horses
once or twice got set, & cast &c– we have had a deal
of bad luck— There is a great many travellers here–
the house is full– – The young Dr told me he was
married, to day— I like him rather better than I did,
before, & ventured to walk on a mile or two with
him– He gave me the history of his courtship &c–
and some information respecting the part of Ohio
he is going to, that was quite interesting— Susan
chose to ride down the hill, & I outwalk'd Mrs W,
so we were quite alone till we reach'd this house– Mrs
Jackson & Eliza had gone on before us, and I every
moment expected to overtake them, but did not see
them till we got here— I am very tir'd & have
laughed myself into a headache; so I can write no
more to night.

Monday morn– Last night we were again cheated
out of our beds, & oblig'd to pass the night as we
could, & that was most uncomfortably– I was quite

unwell with the headache, & had waited for a bed an hour & a half longer than I felt able to set up; & when I found I could get none, I had a long crying spell— This morning I feel almost sick— M^r W— is so much afraid of making trouble, that he will wait till every body else is served, & let them cheat him out of his eyes, & say nothing. Our party here consists of English, Irish, German, & Americans– 2 of the first– 4 of the second– 1 of the third– & a house full of the last— This strange man is an everlasting talker– He knows every body & every thing about them– He has been repeating one of Mr Pierpont Edwards' speeches to me– & one of Mr Hilhouse's– Not one second elapses between his words– He is a very pompous fellow & takes great pains to display what he does know– He has been a schoolmaster– & now I suspect is crazy & running away with a girl he calls his wife– but who seems to be nobody– – It rain'd very fast last night– & is more muddy than ever—

Monday night– a mile west of the mountains–

Rejoice with me my dear Elizabeth, that we are at length over all the mountains, so call'd— I do not suppose we shall be much better off than we were before, as it respects roads– for I had just as lieve go over a mountain, as to go over the same distance of any part of the road we have had this fortnight or three weeks– But it sounds well to say we are over the mountains— We cross'd Chesnut Ridge, the 7th & last M^{tn} this afternoon– It is 5 miles over—12 miles we have come to day— There is a pretty prospect of hills as you come down the M^{tn}— One house on the top of it— We have taken a great deal of pains to get rid of company to day, by going forward & staying behind– but is is an *unpossibility* (Mr Newington) I am more out of patience than ever— We came on to the 4th tavern after we got down,– because we thought those behind us, would stop sooner– Mrs Jackson & her tribe were with us– but we thought all the rest were out of the reach of us– This is a little hut, one window in front– but it is neat & comfortable inside, & we were all quietly seated round the fire, congratulating ourselves on our escape, when in came the young doctor– I thought we should all scream out– Mrs Jackson told him she thought we had lost him– he said he lik'd not to have found us– I wish with all my heart, they had got fast in the mud a little while. The rattlebrain'd fellow is not here, to talk us to death— He pass'd us on the road, singing & screaming, advising us to go back & learn hog latin– alias German– or dutch— We are now 41 miles from Pitt——

Nov^{br} 21st Tuesday Night–A mile from
Greensburg–Penn–

We have had better roads to day, but only came 10 miles— Last night we had good beds, but were oblig'd to sleep in the room with the D^r & his father– M^r & M^{rs} W– of course, as we have determin'd not to sleep out of their room again— The landlord & his wife were extremely clever– they gave us a great many apples & some cherry bounce– Such treatment, after being refus'd even the privilege of getting any victuals,– as we were the night before, was very welcome–– The landlord has been a waggoner– "Only look at that now"–A clever waggoner! I cannot but think his cleverness (is there such a word?) came after he gave up his waggon– – After riding a little way, we overtook Mr Smith again, & found he had been fighting with a waggoner, who began to insult him, by calling him a damn'd Yankee– before they ended M^r S– whipt 3 of them– I was glad they got whipt, for almost every one deserves it–– M^r S– lamented we were not there to see the fun– He declar'd, or rather swore, he would not leave us again, but would stand by and fight for all– He lets his wife ride alone, & he walks on to talk to every one that will listen to him–– As for the D^r, he is "nothing but a pester"– Susan & I took a great deal of pains to go either before or behind to get rid of his company, but it does no good, for he will either wait, or walk faster– I had a great mind to ask him, if he expected to lose his wife soon– We pass'd thro Greensburg, a pretty little town, situated on a high hill– the other waggons had gone on, & were bating in the town– but M^r W– did not stop, so the D^r follow'd on & left his father, & waited at another place for us to bait– We were only able to come a mile farther, as the horses fail'd– The rest of the company had gone on, expecting us to follow– The D^r came in here with us & I thought intended to stay, by his actions, but he at length

A JOURNEY TO OHIO

walk'd on to join the rest of his company— We have
escap'd hearing Mr S– talk, which I would not be
oblig'd to do for 9 pence an hour–

Wednesday morn– I have not spent so pleasant
an evening this long time as the last– Will you believe me, when I tell you we heard some waggoners
conversing upon religious subjects– instead of swearing & cursing– One is an Irish waggoner, & appears
to be sensible, well inform'd man– & what is more,
has read his bible– 2 clever waggoners! I think I
will never condemn a whole race again– I can now,
even believe it possible to find a clever Dutchman in
Pennsylvania. I hope we shall lose all our company this morning– but I expect they will wait for
us– This is a good tavern– We have had sun shine for
2 days past– The weather, as it respects heat & cold,
is very variable– but it invariably rains every day—

Thursday Morn– Sewel's tavern–

Versailes–township–

Yesterday morning, we did not set out till quite
late, but had the good fortune to overtake all our
company within an hour or two, & were oblig'd once
more to put up with them– We had also, a considerable addition to our party— We were oblig'd to
walk a great deal, & just at night, I happen'd to be
on before the waggon some distance & prevented Mr
W– from stopping at a private house, which we
pass'd– I did not think of his wishing it till Mrs J–
mentioned it, I then set out to return, but saw the
waggon coming & sat down on a log– We did not

[55]

reach a tavern till some time after dark– & Mr W–
got hurt & his waggon got set–, & he feels unpleas-
antly towards me, & thinks me the whole cause of
his trouble— The whole family feel & treat me dif-
ferently this morning, & I can not think myself to
blame– for we are oblig'd to walk almost all the time,
& if we are behind the waggon Mr W– always is
angry— Mrs W– Susan & I, were oblig'd to walk,
till we found a house, & if the young Dr had not
been with us, I don't know but we should have pass'd
the night in the woods – but he was so good as to
assist us – The gentlemen all reach'd the tavern before us, & when Mr W– came & told his trouble, they
very kindly went back & assisted him— There were
but two beds to be had, so Mr Smith gave up his
place to me, & Mr & Mrs W took the other— The
gentlemen were very noisy all night, as they could
not lie down— I am much better pleas'd with Mr &
Mrs Smith, than I was before– He is a lawyer– & I
believe knows more, than I at first suspected—   He
is a great talker, & has a story for everything– We
came 14 miles yesterday— To day I am so dreadfully lame that every step I take, almost brings
tears– my feet are sore with walking–

Nov–24– Friday morn– Turtle Creek–Penn–

One misfortune follows another, and I fear we
shall never reach our journey's end—   Yesterday
we came about 3 miles— After coming down an
awful hill, we were oblig'd to cross a creek; but
before we quite came to it, the horses got mired, &

[56]

we expected every moment one of them would die–
but Erastus held his head out of water, while Mr W–
was attempting to unharness them, & Mrs W– &
Susan were on the bank, calling for help— I sat by,
to see the horse breathe his last; but was happily
disappointed in my expectation— No assistance
could be got– till Mr W– waded though the water,
& then 2 men with 3 horses came over— We came
to this Inn, & Mr W– thought it best to stay till this
morning– All our company have gone on– Mr Smith
invited me to ride with his wife, on to Pitts'g– & I on
some accounts, wish I had accepted his invitation–
indeed I could scarcely get beside it—

We found a gentleman (Doctor I presume by his
looks–) here, who was very sociable & staid an hour
with us– He appear'd to be a man of good information & considerable politeness — We found the landlord very good natur'd & obliging, & his wife directly
the contrary— We find the men generally, much
more so than their wives— We are 12 miles from
Pitt——& here like to be– The landlord offers to
keep Susan & me, till spring, & let the old folks go
on— We got into the slough of Despond yesterday–
& are now at the foot of the hill Difficulty– which is
half a mile long– one waggon is already fast in the
mud on it– & Mr W– is afraid to attempt it himself— I think I will winter here——

Friday eve– 9 miles past Pitts'g– Penn–

This morning we set out once more & proceeded 4
miles– It was snowing very fast, & one of our horses

was taken sick & could scarcely get that little distance– Mr W– was oblig'd to whip it almost every
step to keep it from lying down–– We could not
ride at all & stopt at the first tavern we came to––
We are afraid the horse will die & then what will
become of us?–––– I am more than ever discouraged–

Sat– morn– Our horse is better & we are going to
set out again––––

Novbr 26– Saturday night– 3 1-2 miles
beyond Pittsburg–

Just as we were getting into the waggon this morning, Mr W– found he had left his great coat 4 miles
back, & went back on foot after it, while we proceeded to Pittg– which we reach'd about noon–– Mr
W– came about an hour after– – After getting well
warm, Susan & I were going out to view the town,
when Mr W– came & hurried us away, as he wished
to cross the river before night– From the little we
did see of the town, I was extremely disappointed
at its appearance– It is not one half as large as I
suppos'd– but I am unable to give you any account
of it, from my own observation–– It is situated at
the confluence of the 2 rivers, the Alleghany, &
Monongahela– The town suffer'd very much by the
flood– One house floated down the river– its inhabi-
tants were in the upper part of it calling for assistance– none could be render'd & what became of them
I did not learn– I believe it is not known– It was
late before we could cross the river (Alleghany) &

we came on but 3 miles & a half to a very good tavern– The man & his wife are both good natur'd— We found the road to day, better than for a long time— We left almost all the stones when we cross'd the last mountain– & to day I believe we have cross'd the last hills of any consequence– We are now– "on the banks of the pleasant Ohio"——

Sunday eve– It has been all day & still is, raining another flood I fear– All the men in the neighborhood came here to keep the sabbath by drinking whiskey &c &c– but no swearing— I sat reading very quietly & one of them came & desir'd to look over me– I very much doubted whether he could read, but he convinc'd me he could by his observations, which were given with such a tobacco breath as almost suffocated me– He was not more than half shaved, & could read without spelling more than half the words– for he would read a page & half in an hour, nearly— There is a sweet little boy here about 3 years old– He has been writing with me some time & talks so much to me that I am as slow writing as this man was reading— This is the 6th sabbath since I left you— We have lost our company— I quite want to see some of them again—

Wednesday Nov– 28– 7 miles from
Greersburg–Penn–

I have had no opporty of writing you for 3 days– before now– We set out in the rain on Monday, & came on 13 miles– to a hut– with a sign up call'd a tavern– & such a place !– I found the people belong'd

to a very ancient & noble family— They were first &
second cousins to his *Satanic Majesty*— I could but
wonder that he should suffer them to lead so labori-
ous a life, for they are among his most faithful
friends & subjects— Probably they are more useful
to him in that station, by increasing the number of
his subjects— Their dwelling resembles that of their
royal cousin- for it is very dark & gloomy & only
lighted by a great fire- No one who is once caught
in it, ever wishes to be again—   The man is only
related by marriage to his lordship——

Wednesday eve—

The house had only one room in it— There was
a number of travellers & we got but one bed- that
was straw or something harder- The pillow case had
been on 5 or 6 years I *reckon,* so I pin'd over my
handkerchief- & put night gown over my frock—
We rose an hour before day break, got breakfast &
set out in the snow for another hut- We rode several
miles on the Northern bank of the Ohio- We saw
a very large rock containing a great many names-
we added ours to the number— The road was at the
foot of a very high hill or mountain, & so near the
river, there was scarcely room for a waggon- I rode
in constant fear, for the bank down to the river, was
very high and steep— We came on 12 miles, to
Beaver town, on Tuesday- We cross'd the big
Beaver, a stream which empties into the Ohio- It is
generally, fordable, but is at present so rais'd by the
rain, that a flat is used— We found a very good Inn

A JOURNEY TO OHIO

at Beaver town; & soon after supper, Judge Austin & a Mr Weatherby (Merchant–) of Warren, came in—Not Dobson nor Stephenson)— I felt as glad to see them & as well acquainted with them in a few minutes, as if we had all our lives been neighbors— The Judge, resembles Dr Goodsel in his looks;– but is older & larger– Mr Weatherby looks like T. Devereaux— They both, told me they were sorry Mr Edwards did not know I was on the road, that he might have sent an horse after me— They were on their way to Pittg but Judge A, had some idea of returning immediately back to Warren, & they had a mind to hire a horse & have me return with him, but Mr Wolcott objected— I can guess his reason for it, but I will not write it— I very much wish'd it, as I fear I shall be oblig'd to walk a good part of the way- Mr W- says it would not hurt any of us to walk 9 miles every day of our lives- I told him I should not like to walk it in stormy weather, as we are now oblig'd to; but he said it would not hurt me if I shouldn't— I have already worn out my boots almost entirely, with walking— Mr W- is a very strange man- I don't know what to make of him —I shall be so thankful to get thro'– & then if I am caught with a Deacon of any name, again, I shall deserve to suffer— We are within 40 miles of Warren, & to be unable to get there under 4 or 5 days, is perfectly tantalizing— We came 10 1-2 miles to day, & are at a very comfortable Inn, just in the edge of Greersburg- We expected to get a little further, to Hart's tavern quite in the town; & there I hop'd to see Judge Austin again, & I determin'd at any rate to accept his offer of getting me a horse, & go directly on with him, for I do not intend to walk 9 miles a day till we get there, if I can help it– even if it will not hurt me— I won't take the *good* deacon's word for that. The horses are really tir'd out & out, & every day by the time we get 4 miles they will stop & it is extremely difficult to get them on at all– but it is so *expensive* hiring a horse to go on, that as long as the waggon alone, can be drawn 3 or 4 miles a day, it will not be done—but I feel provoked, as you will easily see, so I will write no more on this subject– – I am so anxious to end my journey, that I have lost all interest about the country I pass through— it snows or rains every day, constantly— I think in good weather, the ride from Warren to Pittsᵍ must be pleasant– If that were at present the case, my journal would be as much more interesting, as my journey would be pleasanter— I am quite tir'd of both, but still so habituated to them, that I think it will seem very strange for a few days after I end them, (if I *live* after that time) not to run out the waggon as soon as I have eaten my breakfast—& not to have my journal in my workbag to fill it up— It is very troublesome I assure you— I fear it will be worn out before you get it– it is already very dirty, & so badly written you will never read half of it—

Thursday eve–

10 miles as usual has been our days ride— I have

not walk'd my 9 miles, but I walk'd as much as I could– We are in a comfortable house before an excellent fire– It is snowing very fast—

Saturday– P M– WARREN– After so long a time—

Friday morning we set out early with the hope of getting to Youngstown at night & to Warren to night, but 4 miles from Y——n, the horses were so tir'd they would not stir, so we stopt at a private house for the night, an hour before sun down— We had been in the house but a little time, when Susan look'd out & told me she thought there was some one after me, & I soon saw Mr Edwards & 2 horses— "I was never so happy I think"— I ran out to meet him– He came in & set a while, & just at dark we started for Youngstown—   Mr Edwards insisted upon Susan's going with us, so she rode behind him, and I rode the single horse— We reach'd *Cousin* Joseph Woodbridge's about the middle of the eve— They got us a good supper & gave us a bed— M^{rs} W– is a very pretty woman (I mean pleasing)– They have 3 children, & appear to be very well off, (you understand me) & happy— They live in a very comfortable log house, pleasantly situated– A cousin in this country, is not to be slighted I assure you– I would give more for one in this country, than for 20 in old Connecticut— This morning Mrs Todd came over to see us, & urg'd us to stay & spend the day with her— But spite of her solicitations, we set out for Warren soon after breakfast— My horse was extremely dull & we did not get here till near 2 oclock— Cousin Louisa was as happy to see me as I could wish, & I think I shall be very happy & contented— The town is pleasanter than I expected– The house better– & the children as fine— Cousin has alter'd very little, in any way —I found a Mrs Waldo here just going to Connecticut, & lest I should not have another opport^y, I intend sending this by them, without even time to read it over & correct it— I *am* asham'd of it My dear Elizabeth, & were it not for my promise to you, I don't know that I should dare to send it— I will write your Mama by mail, I have not time for a letter now— My very best love to every body— I have a great deal more to say, but no more time than just to tell you, I am ever

        & most affect^{ly} Yours–

        M V D——

Let no one see this but your own family—